night feeds
and
morning
songs

ABOUT THE AUTHOR

Ana Sampson is the author of many bestselling anthologies including *I Wandered Lonely as a Cloud and Other Poems You Half-Remember from School*, *Tyger Tyger Burning Bright: Much Loved Poems you Half-Remember*, *Poems to Learn by Heart*, *Green* and *Pleasant Land: Best-Loved Poems of the British Countryside* and *Best-Loved Poems: A Treasury of Verse*.

Ana grew up in Kent and studied English Literature at the University of Sheffield. After achieving both a BA and an MA, she began a career in publishing PR and has appeared multiple times on radio and television discussing books and poetry. Ana lives in Surrey with her husband, two daughters and two demanding cats.

night feeds

and

morning
songs

Ana Sampson

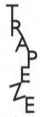

First published in Great Britain in 2021 by Trapeze
This paperback edition published in 2023 by Trapeze
an imprint of The Orion Publishing Group Ltd
Carmelite House, 50 Victoria Embankment
London EC4Y 0DZ

An Hachette UK Company

1 3 5 7 9 10 8 6 4 2

A CIP catalogue record for this book is
available from the British Library.

ISBN (Mass Market Paperback) 978 1 3987 0241 7
ISBN (eBook) 978 1 3987 0242 4

Typeset by Born Group
Printed in Great Britain by Clays Ltd, Elcograf S.p.A

www.orionbooks.co.uk

To my mother, and my daughters, and all the women who walked this way with me –
you know who you are

CONTENTS

❧ Pregnancy ❧

Sleep

The Women
Who Save You

Where Are You?

Milestones

Introduction

It goes without saying – though say it I will – that every pregnancy and every birth, every mother and every child is unique. And yet, despite the fact that my once wakeful newborns are now both fully fledged schoolgirls, and I have neither a hefty teenage son nor an empty nest, each and every one of the poems in this collection told me something profound, devastating or beautiful about motherhood.

In these verses I found a literary incarnation of the community that is so essential to this delicious, brutal, exasperating, exhilarating job of motherhood. This confederacy convenes in draughty church halls, in potty-mouthed WhatsApp groups and at the school gates. Its alliances are forged in waiting rooms and office kitchens, over the tambourines at toddler music classes and at the chipped tables of soft play centres. These tribes sustain us: they cheerlead, they advise, they sympathise. They put the kettle on and pass the good biscuits. They make us feel that we are not alone – and not mad, although what is asked of us as mothers sometimes seems to be. I edited this collection during lockdown, a time that frayed the threads binding us together and physically distanced many of us from our networks of love and support. The fellow feeling I experienced reading these urgent, ecstatic, sometimes heart-squeezing verses held a new poignancy in those strange, lonely days.

These poets take us from the deeply peculiar state of pregnancy, when our children roll and swim within us, to the moments in which we watch them set sail, their eyes on the horizon as we shrink behind them on the shore. And everything in between is here, too, from the tempest of the labour room through the apparently endless hours of sleeplessness (shhhh, shhhh …) to the tying of tiny shoes.

Poetry was a luxurious comfort to me during the newborn days when my bone-deep exhaustion rendered reading a novel a wild and distant fantasy. It was something I could gulp down during a night feed, or while liquidising a blameless vegetable. These poems granted me windows into other dark bedrooms and, when I read about infant-speed toddles, as in Kate Clanchy's beautiful 'The View', I could see something of our own haphazard progress reflected there. As the years passed, I squirrelled away more of these verses. In the company of these poets, I could forgive myself the piled laundry, the toast-for-tea, the 'not-now-I'm-busy's and the school-run screeching. They helped me to approach some of the tender feelings often buried under the avalanche of weaning or wiping, cheering or chivvying, and give them a moment – those quiet moments that are, for some years, so few and precious – to be felt. These women invite us into their homes and their hearts, and we understand ourselves – and this deep, wild, ever-evolving bond – better for hearing their voices.

Every mother is magnificent. These are for you.

Delicious Babies

Because of spring there are babies everywhere,
sweet or sulky, irascible or full of the milk of human
kindness.
Yum, yum! Delicious babies!
Babies with the soft skins of babies, cheeks
of such tit-bit pinkness, tickle-able babies, tasty babies,
mouth-watering babies.

The pads of their hands! The rounds
of their knees! Their good smells of bathtime
and new clothes and gobbled rusks!
Even their discarded nappies are worthy of them,
reveal their powers.
Legions and hosts of babies! Babies bold as lions,
sighing babies,
tricksy babies, omniscient babies, babies using a
plain language

of reasonable demands and courteous acceptance.
Others have the habit of loud contradiction,
can empty a railway carriage (though their displeasing
howls
cheer up childless women).
Look at this baby, sitting bolt upright in his buggy!
Consider his lofty unsmiling acknowledgement of
our adulation,

look at the elfin golfer's hat flattering his fluffy hair!
Look next at this very smallest of babies
tightly wrapped in a foppery of blankets.
In his high promenading pram he sleeps sumptuously,
only a nose, his father's, a white bonnet and a wink
of eyelid showing.

All babies are manic-serene, all babies are mine,
all babies are edible, the boys taste best.
I feed on them, nectareous are my babies,
manna, confiture, my sweet groceries.

I smack my lips,
deep in my belly the egg ripens,
makes the windows shake,
another ovum-quake
moves earth, sky and me …

Bring me more babies! Let me have them for breakfast,
lunch and tea! Let me feast, let my honey-banquet babies
go on forever, fresh deliveries night and day!

Penelope Shuttle

Singing Lando Lullabies

Singing Lando lullabies to you,
Orlando, Orlando,
your eyelids soft while I dream
of the last holiday
two days in Lille, holding hands and
sleeping all night in ironed, white sheets, undisrupted.
He kissed my hair going out to dinner,
dark green dress against the dark blue night air,
with heels tripping over the cobbles of the old town.
Seven courses and marble stairs and glistening glass.
They made a special effort not to serve blue cheese,
so that you were safe.
And on the train, through the streets,
eating chips at lunch,
and delicate meats at dinner,
we talked about your name.
Felix Lexington;
Too many 'xs'.
Orlando Lexington;
too many American places.
Lexington after the pub in Kings Cross
where we met on the dance floor.
I wanted Leonard,
He wanted Ulysses.
I mentioned how handsome he would look

if his name was Orlando.
And I think about how handsome you are now;
my little Lando.

Katharine Perry

Orbit of Three

Planets and stars understand
the luxury of love creating
me from my own materials
like God breathing flowers
from the seeded dust. As
abundant blue earth depends
on the sun, I am to you. You
water me. Eye-light leapt the
red boundaries of blood, stain –
glassed my heart; turned the
deaf *thud thud* counting life's
hurrying hours into drums,
duets, urging me on, on.

And we have made a moon,
out of nothing, like magicians
learning God's best trick.

Gillian Ferguson

White Asparagus

Who speaks of strong currents
streaming through the legs, the breasts
of a pregnant woman
in her fourth month?

She's young, this is her first time,
she's slim and the nausea has gone.
Her belly's just starting to get rounder
her breasts itch all day,

and she's surprised that what she wants
is *him*
     inside her again
Oh come like a horse, she wants to say,
move like a dog, a wolf,
              become a suckling lion-cub –

Come here, and here, and here –
but swim fast and don't stop.

Who speaks of the green coconut uterus
the muscles sliding, a deeper undertow
and the green coconut milk that seals
her well, yet flows so she is wet
from his softest touch?

Who understands the logic
behind this desire?
Who speaks of the rushing tide
                    that awakens
her slowly increasing blood –?
And the hunger
                    raw obsessions beginning
with the shape of the asparagus:
sun-deprived white and purple-shadow-veined,
she buys three kilos
of the fat ones, thicker than anyone's fingers,
she strokes the silky heads
some are so jauntily capped …
            even the smell pulls her in –

Sujata Bhatt

Heartsong

I heard your heartbeat.
It flew out into the room, a startled bird
whirring high and wild.

I stopped breathing to listen
so high and fast it would surely race itself
down and fall

but it held strong, light
vibrant beside the slow deep booming
my old heart suddenly audible.

Out of the union that holds us separate
you've sent me a sound like a name.
Now I know you'll be born.

Jeni Couzyn

Pregnancy

We met early on. There's an initial, thrilling tick and whirr,
a flutter on a hitherto unsuspected inside edge of me.
There were moments when I was going about my life – it
was still mine then – and nobody but I would know that
my attention was far from the meeting room or train
carriage. I was straining secretly, inner ear cocked, like a
dog vibrating with anticipation, for a wave or a wriggle.
The second semester saw my daughter rolling and
tumbling and, a scan revealed, even playing with her toes.
In the last weeks there was indignant heaving, when a
fist or foot could be seen – to the horror of my child-free
colleagues – threatening to burst out of my bulk.

I still have ghost kicks now. Gas, obviously, but there'll

be a moment as I'm bellowing about shoes to my 4-year-old when I'll suddenly feel the echo of tiny her, flickering in my belly. I can't explain to her why I'm pausing in my shrill school-run tirade but there she is, suddenly, as she was, and I'm transported. Before I thud back down into the now of book bags and morning chaos, there's a glimpse into that time of magical possibility, when you're first madly in love with someone you don't yet know.

From the flood of relief when I saw a tiny ticking bean on an early scan to studying the distances between high street bins in case I had to be sick into them, I found pregnancy a peculiar time. How could it not be? Someone is having hiccups inside you! (Was I the only one who thought anxiously of those world record-holders, hiccupping for twelve years straight, every time this happened?) There was the debilitating but oddly luxurious bone tiredness at the start and the end that had me sinking into unconsciousness by 9pm, and the feeling that you've got one foot in a new life that is still – with a first child – unimaginable.

We began researching a slightly terrifying world of arcane equipment – from buggies to bedding, and from sterilisers to swaddling blankets. My urge towards thrifty nesting did battle with the anxiety about plunging into parenthood without some essential piece of kit, though in the event my babies seem unperturbed by the relative cheapness of their pram. (The two things I have done in my life that made me feel most 'mum' were folding up a buggy and chucking it into a car boot, and putting in earrings while briefing a babysitter. Peak mum.)

The mysteries of the state of pregnancy have captured the imagination of generations of writers, from Anna Laetitia Barbauld addressing 'a little invisible being who is expected soon to become visible' at the dawn of the nineteenth century to Jeni Couzyn, holding her breath to hear her baby's heartbeat. It's time for last trips as a couple – Ikhda Ayuning Maharsi being kicked at the Colosseum, and Katharine Perry navigating the cobbles of Lille – before you need an extra suitcase for the baby gubbins and have to snatch baby-free time together during naps. We look, half shyly, at children of all ages and wonder: what will she be like then? And then? What will it feel like to hold his hand crossing a road, to tuck her into bed, to carry them on my hip instead of within? And, as Liz Berry asks in 'The Steps': 'Who will we be when we come back?' Parents are newborn, too, when their children arrive.

Already looking into an invisible distance, already handing in our resignations from our child-free existence, my fellow parenting class students and I lumbered increasingly slowly around the neighbourhood. We lowered ourselves like hippos into the water of the local lido, chuckling at the panic on the skinny lifeguard's face as he calculated which of our massive frames he would be able to heave out of the water if necessary. We awaited dispatches from the ones who had rudely interrupted these last hazy days by doing the thing we each, privately, thought wouldn't really happen to us – giving birth. We obediently ate our pineapple and sipped our raspberry leaf tea. And we waited.

Poems for the New

1–

we're connecting,
                    foot under my rib.
I'm sore with life!
At night,
                    your toes grow. Inches of the new!
The lion prowls the sky
and shakes his tail for you.
Piece of moon
                    fly by my kitchen window.
And your father comes
riding the lion's back
                    in the dark,
to hold me,
                    you,
                        in the perfect circle of him.

2–

Voluptuous against him, I am
nothing superfluous,
but all –
bones, bark of him, root of him take.
I am round

with his sprouting,
new thing new thing!
He wraps me.
The sheets are white.
My belly has tracks on it–
              hands and feet
are moving
under this taut skin.
In snow, in light,
we are about to become!

Kathleen Fraser

To a Little Invisible Being Who Is Expected Soon to Become Visible

Germ of new life, whose powers expanding slow
For many a moon their full perfection wait, –
Haste, precious pledge of happy love, to go
Auspicious borne through life's mysterious gate.

What powers lie folded in thy curious frame, –
Senses from objects locked, and mind from thought!
How little canst thou guess thy lofty claim
To grasp at all the worlds the Almighty wrought!

And see, the genial season's warmth to share,
Fresh younglings shoot, and opening roses glow!
Swarms of new life exulting fill the air, –
Haste, infant bud of being, haste to blow!

For thee the nurse prepares her lulling songs,
The eager matrons count the lingering day;
But far the most thy anxious parent longs
On thy soft cheek a mother's kiss to lay.

She only asks to lay her burden down,
That her glad arms that burden may resume;
And nature's sharpest pangs her wishes crown,
That free thee living from thy living tomb.

She longs to fold to her maternal breast
Part of herself, yet to herself unknown;
To see and to salute the stranger guest,
Fed with her life through many a tedious moon.

Come, reap thy rich inheritance of love!
Bask in the fondness of a Mother's eye!
Nor wit nor eloquence her heart shall move
Like the first accents of thy feeble cry.

Haste, little captive, burst thy prison doors!
Launch on the living world, and spring to light!
Nature for thee displays her various stores,
Opens her thousand inlets of delight.

If charmed verse or muttered prayers had power,
With favouring spells to speed thee on thy way,
Anxious I'd bid my beads each passing hour,
Till thy wished smile thy mother's pangs o'erpay.

Anna Laetitia Barbauld

Bambino

We are walking inside the Colosseum
looking at the ruin of civilisation
Sometimes I stop my steps
caressing you inside my stomach
       and telling you about the poetic histories
We are not travellers like Bryon in Rome was
but I am trying to make you comfortable
and hoping you are not too tired
because I love walking
       down, up, down from the bus
You are so cool, so calm inside my belly
Sometimes we are dancing together
       in the Centro Storico Napoli
just to see the life, culture-set, Roman
Sometimes we are enjoying gelato Fior di Latte
       and because we are both happy
       you are kicking me once again
Sometimes I just pray: for you, for us, our family
       in Piazza Bellini
Sometimes we are buying some Limoncello
       for your dad and my husband
Sometimes you are very calm when I am crying in my bed
trying to write poems
       and I know that you are my reason for life
       after hearing your heart rate for a hundred years

Please forgive our silliness

Cercare Dio
Il mio bambino

We
are
the children too.

Ikhda Ayuning Maharsi

For a Child Expected

Lovers whose lifted hands are candles in winter,
Whose gentle ways like streams in the easy summer,
Lying together
For secret setting of a child, love what they do,
Thinking they make that candle immortal, those streams
    forever flow,
And yet do better than they know.

So the first flutter of a baby felt in the womb,
Its little signal and promise of riches to come,
Is taken in its father's name;
Its life is the body of his love, like his caress,
First delicate and strange, that daily use
Makes dearer and priceless.

Our baby was to be the living sign of our joy,
Restore to each the other's lost infancy;
To a painter's pillaging eye
Poet's coiled hearing, add the heart we might earn
By the help of love; all that our passion would yield
We put to planning our child.

The world flowed in; whatever we liked we took:
For its hair, the gold curls of the November oak
We saw on our walk;
Snowberries that make a Milky Way in the wood

For its tender hands; calm screen of the frozen flood
For our care of its childhood.

But the birth of a child is an uncontrollable glory;
Cat's cradle of hopes will hold no living baby,
Long though it lay quietly.
And when our baby stirs and struggles to be born
It compels humility: what we began
Is now its own.

For *as the sun that shines through glass*
So Jesus in His Mother was.
Therefore every human creature,
Since it shares in His nature,
In candle-gold passion or white
Sharp star should show its own way of light.
May no parental dread or dream
Darken our darling's early beam:
May she grow to her right powers
Unperturbed by passion of ours.

Anne Ridler

DIY

Don't fret about the damp patch
under the window; the baby won't mind.

She'll not bother her head
about the lagging in the roof-space.

The bare floorboards that bring
the sound of your footsteps

will do her just fine, that crack
in the ceiling will be her first pattern.

She won't lose any sleep over
the missing loft ladder,

the crazed toilet bowl, the stubborn cold tap,
that creosote spilling through the fence.

Listen. Already she outgrows her prison,
drums her heels against its walls,

turns turtle, butts her head, blinks,
opens and closes her mouth.

Sit down, pick up your guitar
and sing to her.

Carole Bromley

Ninth Month

Already you are moving down.

Already your floating head
engaged in the inlet
from where you will head out.

Already the world, the world.

And you are slipping
down, away from my heart.

Victoria Redel

Tempo

In the first month I think
it's a drop in a spider web's
necklace of dew

at the second a hazelnut; after,
a slim Black-eyed Susan demurely folded
asleep on a cloudy day

then a bushbaby silent as sap
in a jacaranda tree, but blinking
with mischief

at five months it's an almost-caught
flounder flapping back
to the glorious water

six, it's a song
with a chorus of basses: seven, five grapefruit
in a mesh bag that bounces on the hip
on a hot morning down at the shops

a watermelon next – green oval
of pink flesh and black seeds, ripe
waiting to be split by the knife

nine months it goes faster, it's a bicycle
pedalling for life over paddocks
of sun
no, a money-box filled with silver half-crowns
a sunflower following the clock
with its wide-open grin
a storm in the mountains, spinning rocks
down to the beech trees
three hundred feet below
– old outrageous Queen Bess's best dress
starched ruff and opulent tent of a skirt
packed with ruffles and lace
no no, I've remembered, it's a map
·of intricate distinctions

purples for high ground burnt umber
for foothills green for the plains
and the staggering blue
of the ocean beyond
waiting and waiting and
aching
with waiting

no more alternatives! Suddenly now
you can see my small bag of eternity
pattern of power
my ace my adventure
my sweet-smelling atom
my planet, my grain of miraculous dust
my green leaf, my feather
my lily my lark
look at her, angels –
this is my daughter.

Lauris Edmond

Grafters

They come into your life, naked,
vulnerable, a mighty force you
have no defence against. They
cry you to attention, graft their
desires on your heart, take sleep
and reason from you and cast
a spell on you which you can't
or won't break.

They strengthen their hold with
every passing year, grafting their
joys and sorrows onto the throbbing
pulse of your life, and their children,
and *their* children, graft on the grafts
of generations until your heart's skin
is patched and stretched and aching
with the love and hurt they bring you.

Norah Hanson

Ultrasound

(for Duncan)

I Ultrasound

Oh whistle and I'll come to ye,
my lad, my wee shilpit ghost
summonsed from tomorrow.

Second sight,
A seer's mothy flicker,
An inner sprite:

this is what I see
with eyes closed;
a keek-aboot among secrets.

If Pandora
could have scanned
her dark box,

and kept it locked –
this ghoul's skull, punched eyes
is tiny Hope's,

hauled silver-quick
in a net of sound,
then, for pity's sake, lowered.

II Solstice

To whom do I talk, an unborn thou,
sleeping in a bone creel.

Look what awaits you:
stars, milk-bottles, frost
on a broken outhouse roof

Let's close the door,
and rearrange
the dark red curtain.

Can you tell the days are opening,
admit a touch more light,
just a touch more?

III Thaw

When we brought you home in a taxi
through the steel-grey thaw
after the coldest week in memory
 – even the river sealed itself –
it was I, hardly breathing,
who came through the passage to our yard
welcoming our simplest things:
a chopping block, the frost –
split lintels; and though it meant a journey
through darkening snow,
arms laden with you in a blanket,
I had to walk to the top of the garden,

to touch, in a complicit
homage of equals, the spiral
trunks of our plum trees, the moss,
the robin's roost in the holly.
Leaning back on the railway wall,
I tried to remember;
but even my footprints were being erased
and the rising stars of Orion
denied what I knew: that as we were
hurled on a trolley through swing doors to theatre
they'd been there, aligned on the ceiling,
        ablaze with concern
for that difficult giving,
before we were two, from my one.

IV   February

To the heap of nappies
carried from the automatic
in a red plastic basket

to the hanging out, my mouth
crowded with pegs;
to the notched prop

hoisting the wash,
a rare flight of swans,
hulls still courying snow;

to spring's hint sailing
the westerly, snowdrops
sheltered by rowans –

to the day of St Bride, the first
sweet-wild weeks of your life
I willingly surrender.

V   Bairnsang

Wee toshie man,
          gean tree and rowan
gif ye could staun
yer feet wad lichtsome tread
granite an saun,
but ye cannae yet staun
sae maun courie tae ma airm
an greetna, girna, Gretna Green

Peedie wee lad
          saumon, siller haddie
gin ye could rin
ye'd rin richt easy-strang
ower causey an carse,
but ye cannae yet rin
sae maun jist courie in
and fashna, fashna, Macrahanish Sand

Bonny wee boy
          peeswheep an whaup
gin ye could sing, yer sang
wad be caller
as a lauchin mountain burn
but ye cannae yet sing
sae maun courie tae ma hert
an grieve nat at aa, Ainster an Crail

My ain tottie bairn
          sternie an lift
gin ye could daunce, yer daunce
wad be that o life itsel,
but ye cannae yet daunce
sae maun courie in my erms
and sleep, saftly sleep, Unst and Yell

VI   Sea Urchin

Between my breast
and cupped hand,
          your head

rests as tenderly
as once I may
          have freighted

water, or drawn
treasure, whole
          from a rockpool

with no premonition
of when next I find one
cast up
          broken.

VII Prayer

Our baby's heart, on the sixteen-week scan
was a fluttering bird, held in cupped hands.

I thought of St Kevin, hands opened in prayer
and a bird of the hedgerow nesting there,

and how he'd borne it, until the young had flown
– and I prayed: this new heart must outlive my own.

Kathleen Jamie

The Steps

And this is where it begins, love –
you and I, alone one last time in the slatey night,
the smell of you like Autumn, soil and bonfire,
that November the fourth feeling inside us.
There can be no truer wedding than this:
your bare hand in mine, my body winded
with pain, as you lead me to the car, to the
soon life. And we are frightened, so frightened –

Who will we be when come back?
Will we remember ourselves?
Will we still touch each other's faces
in the darkness, the white noise of night
spilling over us, and believe there is nothing
we could not know or love?

Liz Berry

Labour Ward Prayer

Give us this day our daily miracle.
Exchange our offering of sweat and tears
and, most of all, of blood,
for new life, crumpled as a new leaf bud.

A child is like a pearl, made of pain
and as we sweat the spiral through again,
there's something holy in this moment now.
The mingled prayers and blasphemies, *I can't, I can't*
become *I can*, become *I must*, because
all life hones down into this single point –

the baby. And here at last she comes –
high perfect cry, eyes closed against the light.
Triumphant, exulting. I wash my hands and leave.
They need me for the miracle next door.

Vicky Thomas

The Tempest

Six floors up, the hospital window
frames rage across the bay.
Out I peer at lightning spears
and surging greys. I cannot
hear trouble outside or beyond

the sound of cow.
'Noise won't help,'
the midwife mutters and quits
my stall. She disapproves
of the *mmmooooooooooo*

that escapes,
trails the corridor,
and, reaching the office,
insists she enter
a lonely note in my hospital file.

Of course, I imagine that entry and scene.
Star of my Act, I watch
my husband, watching me. Composed.
I say, 'If it's a boy, we'll call him Prospero.'
He says, 'We know she's a girl. We agreed
on Grace.'

I bellow and bellow again
when he repeats,
'We agreed.'
I should have agreed
to a different part: not
The Cow and not *The Labourer.*
I want to charge
at the man who plays
The Expectant Father.

Instead,
all fours on the bed,
urgent and mooing, I struggle
for Grace,
who emerges.
Tempest-triumphant,
she pumps her fists.
And roars.

Melinda Kallasmae

Poem for a Daughter

'I think I'm going to have it,'
I said, joking between pains.
The midwife rolled competent
sleeves over corpulent milky arms.
'Dear, you never have it,
we deliver it.'
A judgement the years proved true.
Certainly I've never had you

as you still have me, Caroline.
Why does a mother need a daughter?
Heart's needle, hostage to fortune,
freedom's end. Yet nothing's more perfect
than that bleating, razor-shaped cry
that delivers a mother to her baby.
The bloodcord snaps that held
their sphere together. The child,
tiny and alone, creates the mother.

A woman's life is her own
until it is taken away
by a first particular cry.
Then she is not alone
but part of the premises
of everything there is:
a time, a tribe, a war.
When we belong to the world
we become what we are.

Anne Stevenson

The Birthnight

Dearest, it was a night
That in its darkness rocked Orion's stars;
A sighing wind ran faintly white
Along the willows, and the cedar boughs
Laid their wide hands in stealthy peace across
The starry silence of their antique moss:
No sound save rushing air
Cold, yet all sweet with Spring,
And in thy mother's arms, couched weeping there,
      Thou, lovely thing.

Walter de la Mare

The night before the last day of January

(for Caitlin, b. 31.01.03)

will be remembered by a random few
for having borne it out in sheeted snow
on no exceptional stretch of motorway,
rationing the engine's gas-and-air
to intervals of heat while still more snow
slipped down, unprecedented, otherworldly;

but I'll recall it as the unslept night
before that morning-after when you lay
against my heart on the white of ward-square sheets:
a little snowflake fallen into warmth,
fragile, precise, astoundingly unmelting.

Kona Macphee

A Natal Address to My Child, March 19th 1844

Hail to thy puggy nose, my Darling,
Fair womankind's last added scrap,
That, callow as an unfledg'd starling,
Liest screaming in the Nurse's lap.

No locks thy tender cranium boasteth,
No lashes veil thy gummy eye
And, like some steak gridiron toasteth,
Thy skin is red and crisp and dry.

Thy mouth is swollen past describing
Its corners twisted as in scorn
Of all the Leech is now prescribing
To doctor thee, the newly born.

Sweet little lump of flannel binding,
Thou perfect cataract of clothes,
Thy many folds there's no unwinding
Small mummy without arms or toes!

And am I really then thy Mother?
My very child I cannot doubt thee,
Rememb'ring all the fuss and bother
And moans and groans I made about thee!

'Tis now thy turn to groan and grumble,
As if afraid to enter life,
To dare each whipping scar and tumble
And task and toil with which 'tis rife.

O Baby of the wise round forehead,
Be not too thoughtful ere thy time;
Life is not truly quite so horrid –
Oh! how she squalls! – she can't bear rhyme!

Eliza Ogilvy

Big Boots

For you my mid-rift stretched
like I'd swallowed Army boots.
Breasts bloated
fingers swelled
I developed cankles.
My shoulders grew so broad
they could carry all the shoes
from all the pathways
of the world
for you. I stood
on the shoulders
of the women before:
Mary Ann
Patricia
Phyllis

and I grew tall enough
to never need heels
to see beyond (time)
I grew large enough
to cushion your limbs
wide enough to be
a battering ram
for your foes.

When you flooded from me
pain made me mighty
and fierce
but you split me
in half
made me great
and yet small again.
I looked at your face; crunkled, waxy, squashed
and I was just a tiny ant again, on the surface
of the world, terrified of big boots.

Thommie Gillow and Hannah Teasdale

First Birth

I had thought so little, really, of *her*,
inside me, all that time, not breathing –
intelligent, maybe curious,
her eyes closed. When the vagina opened,
slowly, from within, from the top, my eyes
rounded in shock and awe, it was like being
entered for the first time, but entered
from the inside, the child coming in
from the other world. Enormous, stately,
she was pressed through the channel, she turned, and rose,
they held her up by a very small ankle,
she dangled indigo and scarlet, and spread
her arms out in this world. Each thing
I did, then, I did for the first
time, touched the flesh of our flesh,
brought the tiny mouth to my breast,
she drew the avalanche of milk
down off the mountain, I felt as if
I was nothing, no one, I was everything to her, I was hers.

Sharon Olds

And

suddenly you are here
and I am astonished
by the way you smell of bloody bread
and the way you already decide
to place a webbed hand here,
to slow-wink a newt's eye there.
I am astonished that you are purple.

And now I know glee
at the indignant heaving bellows of your belly,
your self-startled arms flung wide proclaiming
your tiny chimp gums.

And I watch to see time
measured by your face,
crane as you push each new word through glottal air.
I thrill because you're not like me
but you and young and other.

Christy Ducker

Welcome Wee One

O ma darlin wee one
At last you are here in the wurld
And wi' aa your wisdom
Your een bricht as the stars,
You've filled this hoose with licht,
Yer trusty wee haun, your globe o' a heid,
My cherished yin, my hert's ain!

O ma darlin wee one
The hale wurld welcomes ye:
The mune glowes; the hearth wairms.
Let your life hae luck, health, charm,
Ye are my bonny blessed bairn,
My small miraculous gift.
I never kent luve like this.

Jackie Kay

Her First Week

She was so small I would scan the crib a half-second
to find her, face-down in a corner, limp
as something gently flung down, or fallen
from some sky an inch above the mattress. I would
tuck her arm along her side
and slowly turn her over. She would tumble
over part by part, like a load
of damp laundry, in the dryer, I'd slip
a hand in, under her neck,
slide the other under her back,
and evenly lift her up. Her little bottom
sat in my palm, her chest contained
the puckered, moire sacs, and her neck –
I was afraid of her neck, once I almost
thought I heard it quietly snap,
I looked at her and she swivelled her slate
eyes and looked at me. It was in
my care, the creature of her spine, like the first
chordate, as if the history
of the vertebrate had been placed in my hands.
Every time I checked, she was still
with us – someday, there would be a human
race. I could not see it in her eyes,
but when I fed her, gathered her

like a loose bouquet to my side and offered
the breast, greyish-white, and struck with
minuscule scars like creeks in sunlight, I
felt she was serious, I believed she was willing to stay.

Sharon Olds

Something

Resting her on my chest like a sleeping cat
I cannot recall my older daughter so small and new
and fear the memory of this
complete, absolute *something* will grow away
and fear the hand will never remember
stroking her head as she nursed
or fear I'll forget her soft cry
when I look up from sleep and see you lift her,
4am, the curtains blowing in and out of the window
as the whole house breathes.

Kimiko Hahn

When Six O'Clock Comes
and Another Day Has Passed

the baby who cannot speak, speaks to me.
When the sun has risen and set over the same dishes
and the predicted weather is white cloud,
the baby steadies her head which is the head of a drunk
and holds me with her blue eyes,
eyes which have so recently surfed through womb-swell,
and all at once we stop half-heartedly row, rowing
our boat and see each other clear
in the television's orange glow. She regards me,
the baby who does not know a television from a table lamp,
the baby, who is so heavy with other people's hopes
she has no body to call her own,
the baby who is forever being shifted, rearranged,
whose hands must be unfurled and wiped with cotton wool,
whose scalp must be combed of cradle cap,
the baby who has exactly no memories
softens her face in the early evening light and says
   I understand.

Kathryn Simmonds

Young Mother

There is no schedule. Like the baby,
I am untethered and unknowing. I
wear the baby like a spare appendage.
In these years it is in vogue to choose
a kind of mothering – attachment or
otherwise. I choose a pacing tiger, a
milk-drained spud. I wear my heart
like a too-big sleeve, dragging it across
every surface. In the evenings when
the world bares its ugly teeth – we walk.
Down sidewalks and stairs, hallways
and the rim of crowded rooms. When
someone asks for my ambitions, there
is no answer. I only dream of sleep.

Kate Baer

Sleep

I no longer inhabit the crazed kingdom of sleeplessness.

(I leave here a judicious pause, for you to retrieve this book if you have – quite understandably – just hurled it at the wall.)

But I remember well the shattering dominion it held over me. Besides, I kept a sporadic diary. It reads like a mad woman's scrawling on the attic walls, each day an obsessive litany of times: 'Up at 1.30am, 3.40am and again at 4.30am … but not for long! Not too bad!' I scribble at one point with desperate jollity. I was searching, like an obsessive alchemist, for the magic formula. (No pun intended.)

There were mornings – none more so than that first one in the hospital – when daylight felt like a miracle. 'We did it!' I burbled at the nonplussed woman who brought me cornflakes. Like my daughter, I was hungry and thirsty all the time, so my phone occasionally sustained mild nocturnal brie damage. I would sometimes wake in a panic, especially early on, having dreamed that I'd lost the baby somewhere, neatly stashed in an overhead locker or packed tidily away into a drawer. Despite my happiness, exhaustion and the shock of the new could make everything feel hallucinated. I learned that high expectations – of myself, of experiences, of my child, of my ability to make it into town to visit the aquarium – were not my friends. I can think with a smile now of the ambitious plans – to be honest, verging on the Dickensian – I had for my baby's first Christmas. There would surely be carol-singing, bracing walks and relaxed feasts at which my daughter would delight the family by beaming from her highchair! In the event, it was lovely … but my husband and I spent most of it sleeping in shifts, shuffling past each other occasionally on the stairs.

Word passed among the mothers, in the playgrounds and the weighing rooms, of fool-proof paths to our most cherished fantasy: five solid hours. As Kate Baer admits in 'Young Mother', 'I only dream of sleep'. We had to believe that the white noise apps and recorded lullabies, the dimly lit and lavender-scented bath-time incantations, the mathematics of milk, or some complicated combination of all these, would grant us rest. I developed a fervent but entirely misplaced confidence in the power of the word 'shhhhhhhh'. For at least a year, I found it hard to stand without bobbing soothingly, even when my arms were empty. Those whose babies slept well – even if only for a week – tactfully fell silent as the rest of us pored over schemes and books, folklore and rumours, like a desperate council of war. A friend of mine, eyes wide, said it best. In a horrified whisper, she confided: *'There is no night.'*

The wholesome meals I had imagined producing with all the extra time at my disposal during my maternity leave did not materialise. I ate anything I could extract (preferably one-handed) from its packaging and put straight into my mouth. (My top tip for a dish that works at any meal? Quiche. It's breakfasty *enough*, right?) Half-awake, I bumbled through household tasks, once forgetting to remove the soothing cabbage leaves from my bra and accidentally making vegetarian baby-clothing soup in the washing machine. Somebody told me: 'Never stand when you can sit, never sit when you can lie.' But I didn't need to be told by then. I existed, running on fumes, in a delirious fug of fatigue.

And nobody told me they would be so LOUD. My beautiful baby made noises akin to a drunken Dobermann when she eventually slumbered. And when she was silent, I was prickling with vigilance – sometimes even when I was, technically, asleep – ready for the howl. 'My sleep floats within a listening,' writes Alice B. Fogel in 'If I Sleep while My Baby Sleeps' – a perfect encapsulation of that dim and eerie halfway state. I heard legends about infants who gurgled or chuntered when they woke, who awaited their parents' entrance in the mornings lying with a sunny smile in the cot. Mine seemed to start bellowing as a pre-emptive measure before she was fully awake. If she had been an irritating colleague, *all* her emails would have been marked urgent. I couldn't imagine ever not being wrenched out of sleep, panicking, on the sharp point of a scream again. The only conclusions I drew, and the only pieces of advice I feel qualified to give, are these. Firstly, there are no answers. And secondly: this, too, shall pass.

There are some beautiful poems here about babies at night. Unsurprisingly, they aren't about the screaming. Swaddled and sleeping-bagged, they settle on chests, they call from their cots, they are turned over 'part by part', as Sharon Olds does in 'Her First Week', with infinite care and lowered with breath held – *don't wake, don't wake, don't wake*. Through the exhaustion, despite the perpetual longing for just one more hour's sleep, there are poets here who exult in that quiet moment when the world is no bigger than the two of you in the dark, and tiny feet and hands – busy all day – are, as Edith Nesbit's 'Song' beautifully promises us, still enough to hold.

Night Feed

This is dawn.
Believe me
This is your season, little daughter.
The moment daisies open,
The hour mercurial rainwater
Makes a mirror for sparrows.
It's time we drowned our sorrows.

I tiptoe in.
I lift you up
Wriggling
In your rosy, zipped sleeper.
Yes, this is the hour
For the early bird and me
When finder is keeper.

I crook the bottle.
How you suckle!
This is the best I can be,
Housewife
To this nursery
Where you hold on,
Dear life.

A silt of milk.
The last suck.
And now your eyes are open,
Birth-coloured and offended.
Earth wakes.
You go back to sleep.
The feed is ended.

Worms turn
Stars go in.
Even the moon is losing face.
Poplars stilt for dawn
And we begin
The long fall from grace.
I tuck you in.

Eavan Boland

Morning Song

Love set you going like a fat gold watch.
The midwife slapped your footsoles, and your bald cry
Took its place among the elements.

Our voices echo, magnifying your arrival. New statue.
In a drafty museum, your nakedness
Shadows our safety. We stand round blankly as walls.

I'm no more your mother
Than the cloud that distills a mirror to reflect its own slow
Effacement at the wind's hand.

All night your moth-breath
Flickers among the flat pink roses. I wake to listen:
A far sea moves in my ear.

One cry, and I stumble from bed, cow-heavy and floral
In my Victorian nightgown.
Your mouth opens clean as a cat's. The window square

Whitens and swallows its dull stars. And now you try
Your handful of notes;
The clear vowels rise like balloons.

Sylvia Plath

Sleeping and Watching

Sleep on, baby, on the floor,
    Tired of all the playing:
Sleep with smile the sweeter for
    That, you dropped away in.
On your curls' full roundness stand
    Golden lights serenely;
One cheek, pushed out by the hand,
    Folds the dimple inly:
Little head and little foot
    Heavy laid for pleasure,
Underneath the lids half shut,
    Slants the shining azure.
Open-soul in noonday sun,
    So you lie and slumber:
Nothing evil having done,
    Nothing can encumber.

I, who cannot sleep as well,
    Shall I sigh to view you?
Or sigh further to foretell
    All that may undo you?
Nay, keep smiling, little child,
    Ere the sorrow neareth:
I will smile too! patience mild
    Pleasure's token weareth.
Nay, keep sleeping before loss:

I shall sleep though losing!
As by cradle, so by cross,
    Sure is the reposing.

And God knows who sees us twain,
    Child at childish leisure,
I am near as tired of pain
    As you seem of pleasure.
Very soon too, by His grace
    Gently wrapt around me,
Shall I show as calm a face,
    Shall I sleep as soundly.
Differing in this, that you
    Clasp your playthings, sleeping,
While my hand shall drop the few
    Given to my keeping:
Differing in this, that I
    Sleeping shall be colder,
And in waking presently,
    Brighter to beholder:
Differing in this beside
    (Sleeper, have you heard me?
Do you move, and open wide
    Eyes of wonder toward me?)

Elizabeth Barrett Browning

To the Women Marching, from a Mother at Home

It is cold, and my son is small.
I rock him in the fragile boat of my body
between this night's dark and a brighter shore.

We are always awake.

He curves at my breast like a comma
between the words anchored deep in my chest,
and the breath taking form in his lungs.

In the quiet, we hear your chanting.

Remember us with you, we are the rear-guard.
I am carrying him like banner, feel him
cutting his teeth on my curdled milk.

I am sharpening him like an arrow.

Jen Stewart Fueston

Great-grandmother,

Great-grandmother,

be with us
as if in the one same day & night
we all gave birth
in the one same safe-house, warm,
and then we rest together,
sleep, and nurse,
dreamily talk to our babies, warm,
in a safe room   all of us
carried in the close black sky.

Jean Valentine

The Chair by the Window

Your rhythmic nursing slows. I feel
your smile before I see it: nipple pinched
in corner of mouth, your brimming, short, tuck-cornered
smile. I shake my head, my *no* vibrates
to you through ribs and arms. Your tapered ears
quiver, work faintly and still pinker, my
nipple spins right out and we
are two who sit and smile into each other's eyes.

Again, you frowning farmer, me your cow:
you flap one steadying palm against my breast,
thump down the other, chuckle, snort, and then
you're suddenly under, mouth moving steadily, eyes
drifting past mine abstracted, your familiar
blue remote and window-paned with light.

Anne Winters

The Mother

Here I lean over you, small son, sleeping
Warm in my arms,
And I con to my heart all your dew-fresh charms,
As you lie close, close in my hungry hold …
Your hair like a miser's dream of gold,
And the white rose of your face far fairer,
Finer, and rarer
Than all the flowers in the young year's keeping;
Over lips half parted your low breath creeping
Is sweeter than violets in April grasses;
Though your eyes are fast shut I can see their blue,
Splendid and soft as starshine in heaven,
With all the joyance and wisdom given
From the many souls who have stanchly striven
Through the dead years to be strong and true.

Those fine little feet in my worn hands holden …
Where will they tread?
Valleys of shadow or heights dawn-red?
And those silken fingers, O, wee, white son,
What valorous deeds shall by them be done
In the future that yet so distant is seeming
To my fond dreaming?
What words all so musical and golden
With starry truth and poesy olden

Shall those lips speak in the years on-coming?
O, child of mine, with waxen brow,
Surely your words of that dim to-morrow
Rapture and power and grace must borrow
From the poignant love and holy sorrow
Of the heart that shrines and cradles you now!

Some bitter day you will love another,
To her will bear
Love-gifts and woo her ... then must I share
You and your tenderness! Now you are mine
From your feet to your hair so golden and fine,
And your crumpled finger-tips ... mine completely,
Wholly and sweetly;
Mine with kisses deep to smother,
No one so near to you now as your mother!
Others may hear your words of beauty,
But your precious silence is mine alone;
Here in my arms I have enrolled you,
Away from the grasping world I fold you,
Flesh of my flesh and bone of my bone!

Lucy Maud Montgomery

Never Letting Go

Our bed is attached to our child's
Anonymous nature clouds into our dreams
We lie like three crows,
All our hair falls forward
Dangling swade, like a cliff top
hanging, tilting windmills
holding and
exhausting the wind
Never letting go.
We live in one room,
right in town
and fly eight hours of dawn, in single grey
all of the light rings above the walls.
We never invite anyone in,
we leave less and less.

Greta Bellamacina

Afterthought
(for my daughter)

I am following with my finger the blue veins
that travel from wrist to stoop of palm
as you lie now, little milk-drunk carcass,
in an accident of sleep. This is what mothers do

or what I've learned to do, to search your body
for signs of life, wary of pulse and breath
as all the time you follow me,
your mouth, insistent, through the night.

See! I have pressed the soft vowels of your imagination
and made them part of me. They pull me open, stitch me up,
your animal grunts and hungry gestures –
so much a noise that might come from my own mouth,

I can't tell us apart. When I do, daughter, I'll admit, I'm lost,
my new body wandering the forest,
dropping trails of bright stones
till I find you again, a new friend in an old place.

And for how many nights will it be this way,
this slow process of making and undoing,
the soft osmosis of your fragile body? My willing you not
to slip away, turning my own blue veins

to ice? I watch sand gather at your eyes' corners,
shadows making your face from nothing,
those eyes, which might turn any colour,
flickering, half-open, in the pages of your sleep.

I let them rise inside me, birds cased in glass.
And all the while snow falls, depositing on lawns and roofs
its subtle metamorphic chemistry.
Days drift to your smiles.

And I watch the pink coil of your ear,
the snub nose of beginnings;
count to myself in this lonely country
the hoots of an owl, a line of trees,

the bright rings of your growth.

Deryn Rees-Jones

A Mother to Her Waking Infant

Now in thy dazzling half-oped eye,
Thy curled nose and lip awry,
Thy up-hoist arms and noddling head,
And little chin with crystal spread,
Poor helpless thing! what do I see,
    That I should sing of thee?

From thy poor tongue no accents come,
Which can but rub thy toothless gum;
Small understanding boasts thy face,
Thy shapeless limbs nor step nor grace;
A few short words thy feats may tell,
    And yet I love thee well.

When sudden wakes the bitter shriek,
And redder swells thy little cheek;
When rattled keys thy woes beguile,
And through the wet eye gleams the smile,
Still for thy weakly self is spent
    Thy little silly plaint.

But when thy friends are in distress,
Thou'lt laugh and chuckle ne'er the less;
Nor e'en with sympathy be smitten,
Though all are sad but thee and kitten;
Yet little varlet that thou art,
    Thou twitchest at the heart.

Thy rosy cheek so soft and warm;
Thy pinky hand and dimpled arm;
Thy silken locks that scantly peep,
With gold-tipped ends, where circles deep
Around thy neck in harmless grace
So soft and sleekly hold their place,
Might harder hearts with kindness fill,
    And gain our right goodwill.

Each passing clown bestows his blessing,
Thy mouth is worn with old wives' kissing;
E'en lighter looks the gloomy eye
Of surly sense, when thou art by;
And yet I think whoe'er they be,
    They love thee not like me.

Perhaps when time shall add a few
Short years to thee, thou'lt love me too.
Then wilt thou, through life's weary way
Become my sure and cheering stay;
Wilt care for me, and be my hold,
    When I am weak and old.

Thou'lt listen to my lengthened tale,
And pity me when I am frail –
But see, the sweepy spinning fly
Upon the window takes thine eye.
Go to thy little senseless play –
    Thou dost not heed my lay.

Joanna Baillie

Hare

I kept you in bed with me so many nights,
certain I could hold the life into you,
certain that the life in you wanted to leap out, hare-like,
go bobbing off into some night-field.
For want of more eyes, more arms
I strapped you to me while I did the dishes, cooked, typed,
your little legs frogging
against the deflating dune of your first home.
Nested you in a car seat while I showered, dressed,
and when you breastfed for hours and hours
I learned how to manoeuvre the cup and book around you.
Time and friends and attitudes, too.
We moved breakables a height, no glass tables.
Fitted locks to the kitchen cupboards, door jammers,
argued about screws and pills someone left within reach.
I'll not tell you how my breath left me, how my heart stopped
at your stillness in the cot, and who I became
when at last you moved. There is no telling
what skins of me have dropped and shed in the fears
I've entered. What I will say is that the day
beyond these blankets, beyond our door
is known to me now, fragile as moth-scurf,
its long ears twitching, alert,
white tail winking across the night-field.

Carolyn Jess-Cooke

The Evening Star

Hesperus, you bring everything that
                    the light-tinged dawn has scattered;
you bring the sheep, you bring the goat, you bring
                  the child back to its mother.

Sappho
trans. Josephine Balmer

Night Feeding

Deeper than sleep but not so deep as death
I lay there sleeping and my magic head
remembered and forgot.   On first cry I
remembered and forgot and did believe.
I knew love and I knew evil:
woke to the burning song and the tree burning blind,
despair of our days and the calm milk-giver who
knows sleep, knows growth, the sex of fire and grass,
and the black snake with gold bones.

Black sleeps, gold burns;   on second cry I woke
fully and gave to feed and fed on feeding.
Gold seed, green pain, my wizards in the earth
walked through the house, black in the morning dark.
Shadows grew in my veins, my bright belief,
my head of dreams deeper than night and sleep.
Voices of all black animals crying to drink,
cries of all birth arise, simple as we,
found in the leaves, in clouds and dark, in dream,
deep as this hour, ready again to sleep.

Muriel Rukeyser

If I Sleep while My Baby Sleeps

I will hear his sleep
in and through my own, my sleep
will be bathed in his as if we slept
in one same fluid

My sleep floats within a listening
so deep that the separating
spaces of air become
as pliant and full as snowfall,
its singing silence as profound

My ears and his throat —
the sensation of anticipated
hearing close inside the ear
and the incipient murmur or cry
forming at the end of his sleep —
borne like birds and thrumming
on the air of rooms between us

My own sleep will be his
clock, safely keeping time,
his sleep tunes my dreams to listen,
our sleep binds the hour,
heavy and warm,
into a blanket of air
and sound

Alice B. Fogel

Extract from
On Viewing Her Sleeping Infant

Come, soft babe! with every grace
Glowing in thy matchless face —
Come, unconscious innocence!
Every winning charm dispense —
All thy little arts — thine own —
For thou the world hast never known!
And yet thou canst, a thousand ways,
A mother's partial fondness raise!
And all her anxious soul detain
With many a link of pleasing chain;
Leading captive at thy will,
Following thy little fancies still.
Though nature yet thy tongue restrains,
Nor canst thou lisp thy joys or pains!
Yet every gracious meaning lies
Within the covert of thine eyes:
Wit, and the early dawn of sense,
Live in their silent eloquence.

Maria Frances Cecilia Cowper

Against Dark's Harm

The baby at my breast
suckles me to rest.
Who lately rode my blood,
finds me further flood,
pulls me to his dim
unimagined dream.

Amulet and charm
against dark's harm,
coiled in my side,
shelter me from fright
and the edged knife,
despair, distress
and all self-sickness.

Anne Halley

Song for a Babe

Little babe, while burns the west,
Warm thee, warm thee in my breast;
While the moon doth shine her best,
    And the dews distil not.

All the land so sad, so fair –
Sweet its toils are, blest its care.
Child, we may not enter there!
    Some there are that will not.

Fain would I thy margins know,
Land of work, and land of snow;
Land of life, whose rivers flow
    On, and on, and stay not.

Fain would I thy small limbs fold,
While the weary hours are told,
Little babe in cradle cold.
    Some there are that may not.

Jean Ingelow

Song

Oh, baby, baby, baby dear,
We lie alone together here;
The snowy gown and cap and sheet
With lavender are fresh and sweet;
Through half-closed blinds the roses peer
To see and love you, baby dear.

We are so tired, we like to lie
Just doing nothing, you and I,
Within the darkened quiet room.
The sun sends dusk rays through the gloom,
Which is no gloom since you are here,
My little life, my baby dear.

Soft sleepy mouth so vaguely pressed
Against your new-made mother's breast.
Soft little hands in mine I fold,
Soft little feet I kiss and hold,
Round soft smooth head and tiny ear,
All mine, my own, my baby dear.

And he we love is far away!
But he will come some happy day,
You need but me, and I can rest
At peace with you beside me pressed.
There are no questions, longings vain,
No murmuring, nor doubt, nor pain,
Only content and we are here,
    My baby dear.

Edith Nesbit

Night Light

Only your plastic night light dusts its pink
on the backs and undersides of things; your mother,
head resting on the nightside of one arm,
floats a hand above your cradle
to feel the humid tendril of your breathing.
Outside, the night rocks, murmurs … Crouched
in this eggshell light, I feel my heart
slowing, opened to your tiny flame

as if your blue irises mirrored me
as if your smile breathed and warmed
and curled in your face which is only asleep.
There is space, between me, I know,
and you. I hang above you like a planet –
you're a planet, too. One planet loves the other.

Ann Winters

Ruins

Here's my body
in the bath, all the skin's
inflamed trenches
and lost dominions,

my belly's fallen keystone
its slackened tilt –
for all the Aztec gold
I'd not give up

this room where you slept,
your spine to my right,
your head
stoppered in my pelvis

like a good amen –
amen I say
to my own damn bulk,
my milk-stretched breasts –

amen I say to all of this
if I have you –
your screw-ball smile
at every dawn,

your half-pitched, milk-wild smile
at every waking call,
my loved-beyond-all-reason
darling, dark-eyed girl.

Fiona Benson

The Republic of Motherhood

I crossed the border into the Republic of Motherhood
and found it a queendom, a wild queendom.
I handed over my clothes and took its uniform,
its dressing gown and undergarments, a cardigan
soft as a creature, smelling of birth and milk,
and I lay down in Motherhood's bed, the bed I had made
but could not sleep in, for I was called at once to work
in the factory of Motherhood. The owl shift,
the graveyard shift. Feedingcleaninglovingfeeding.
I walked home, heartsore, through pale streets,
the coins of Motherhood singing in my pockets.
Then I soaked my spindled bones
in the chill municipal baths of Motherhood,
watching strands of my hair float from my fingers.
Each day I pushed my pram through freeze and blossom
down the wide boulevards of Motherhood
where poplars bent their branches to stroke my brow.
I stood with my sisters in the queues of Motherhood –
the weighing clinic, the supermarket – waiting
for Motherhood's bureaucracies to open their doors.
As required, I stood beneath the flag of Motherhood
and opened my mouth although I did not know the anthem.
When darkness fell I pushed my pram home again,
and by lamplight wrote urgent letters of complaint
to the Department of Motherhood but received no response.

I grew sick and was healed in the hospitals of Motherhood
with their long-closed isolation wards
and narrow beds watched over by a fat moon.
The doctors were slender and efficient
and when I was well they gave me my pram again
so I could stare at the daffodils in the parks of Motherhood
while winds pierced my breasts like silver arrows.
In snowfall, I haunted Motherhood's cemeteries,
the sweet fallen beneath my feet –
Our Lady of the Birth Trauma, Our Lady of Psychosis.
I wanted to speak to them, tell them I understood,
but the words came out scrambled, so I knelt instead
and prayed in the chapel of Motherhood, prayed
for that whole wild fucking queendom,
its sorrow, its unbearable skinless beauty,
and all the souls that were in it. I prayed and prayed
until my voice was a nightcry
and sunlight pixelated my face like a kaleidoscope.

Liz Berry

Something wonderful has happened it is called you

And mostly these days I just like to look
at you and sometimes make words
out of your name or rock you
in my arms till the thought of I
with or without poetry
no longer matters.
It's not like I have forgotten
how to worry

– the disappearing forests,
   vanishing species
   zone of sky above our heads –

I pray that when you grow up there may still be
the forests, for instance, and the species

– precious zone of sky
   to keep sun off yr precious face –

And not just in the zoo.
I worry about other things too but mostly
it is hard to be unhappy these days
especially now the spring's advancing
and you're learning
about hands, how to hold things in them
and take everything it's yours.

Emily Critchley

The Baby Who Understood Shadows

She found him, on his front, one arm raised
and conducting the air. Three months old,

his limbs mere feelers on her carpeted home,
until the sun tipped his shadow on the floor:

made a shape impossible to push or pull
and he acted upon it. She believed

he was reaching, that his fingers
wanted to grab, but the shadow

was all there was, dancing
beneath his elbow. He hadn't heard her

come into the room, hadn't flexed
to her milky scent. She watched

as the link between light, object, surface
became coherent to this speechless being.

His eyes followed fist. The fist she held
in her lips, when love required her to eat him

in mouthfuls. This baby she washed, fed,
kept close as fog, now able to see through

the branches of her arms, find the sun's rays,
his own shadow, all things that are not her.

Rebecca Goss

The Call

The Fall winds covered my bed with a sheet of leaves;
drought in much of the country, fires already.
I was dry in my skeleton, old bones
crackling in their sleep beneath the duck down,
dreams like teasing sheep's wool through a dark hole.

I thought I was a member of ordinary time,
two Sundays after the Ascension, or was it the Assumption?
But then she was here, new under the sun;
she examined every leaf, one by one by one;
she rolled on the bed laughing, and I joined in.

Hail to her, and sunlight, and spirit songs.
She bends the back of the wind and lets it go
so it springs forward with a shower of bright stars.
I touch her tiny shoulder blades as a gentle reminder –
she'll be my flown one; I will call after her

and my call will go higher and higher
till it's just air and only dolphins hear it.

Sara Berkeley

The Baby

He who has nothing to hide,
has nothing to show.

- MARGUERITE DE HAINAUT

My baby is playing in the bath, delighted. I begin
to wash his head and spend some time at this.
Then he begins. When I start to rinse his hair, I
can't find him. I turn around, and there he is
again. I don't understand what is happening, and
grow stern. I scold him. I don't like what he's
doing. The baby laughs, more and more amused,
glimmers for an instant, and vanishes again. My
impatience only makes things worse. He disap-
pears more and more quickly, doesn't even give
me time to protest. Through layers of uneasiness,
I glimpse his mischievous glance; my blindness is
his victory, my jealousy his passion. For a while, I
go on resisting: I don't know how to welcome
impotence. The baby just wants to play. The
game is dazzling and lasts a lifetime.

María Negroni
trans. Anne Twitty

The New Mothers

They have mastered the buggy –
they understand the awkward catch,
what force of pressure makes it give.
They wheel with confidence, more
confidence, they wheel through afternoons
of amnesiac light, through mornings
loud with rain and evenings when
the sky is soothed to pink, thinking of
the secrets recently unshelled, the ones
their mothers kept so long, the bloody
songs of sealed rooms which day by day
grow faint and fainter still.
They pass by women being wheeled,
women sinking in their chairs who once
(can it be true?) sat small and snug
in carriage prams. Swelling women
pass by too, manoeuvring their mounds
they seem as far removed as first-year girls
to sixth formers. And of course
they pass their kind, in cafes; parks –
half smiles, shy, as if they saw the nipples weep
inside each other's clothes. Another cup of tea;
they pause and redirect their gaze away,
beyond the complicated child they've made,
beyond the blurred pedestrians to girls

in skinny jeans, remembering how (again
impossibly) they *were* those girls,
the Matryoshka trick that had them
for a minute spotlit, arms raised
to glorify the tiny hours, sweat glittering
their foreheads – white light, noise –
and years away, unreachable through dancefloor mist,
babies with wet mouths feeding in the dark.

Kathryn Simmonds

The Women
Who Save You

The success of a journey depends on your fellow travellers. The poems in this book remind me that we are not alone. Women walked and will walk this way, with their babies cocooned in their buggies or bound to their chests, hundreds of years ago, and yesterday, and tomorrow. They have wiped and kissed, patted and rocked, nagged and cheered, just as we do. Every pregnancy, every birth, every mother and every child is wildly different, but there are so many sensations and emotions I recognise in these pages.

Though most of us cope now without the mythical village that blissed-out blog posts are always harking back to, there are helping hands – particularly from women – that guide and support us along this path. Despite the fact that parenting advice can be a minefield, and much had changed since her own baby-rearing days, I was lucky that my mother was a calming presence. She insisted serenely on my angelic babyhood (in stark contrast, apparently, to my naughty little sister whose childhood nickname was the Demon Queen). A week in, and almost every day since, I have needed to thank my mother for acts of love I can't even remember, as well as all those I can. Belatedly, I express proper gratitude for the honey and lemon drinks and the laundry, for homework supervision and refereeing the sibling battles, for boundless tact and a free taxi service. My no-longer-demonic sister came to my aid in those earliest days too. She eyed the new, raw, mad me with compassionate bafflement and sat with my daughter and me through the sweltering first day of my husband's return to work. My much-loved and missed mother-in-law was so kind, always, and besotted beyond all reason.

The women whose first babies arrived with mine, women I'd only known in our strange newish pregnant state, became immediately, urgently intimate. Our relationships with each other were only a few weeks old, forged during feeding seminars and giggly attempts to swaddle rubbery dolls. We whispered reports from those who had gone before, wide-eyed and incredulous over the particulars: 'Every three hours. *Every. Three. Hours*?' We talked about how we wouldn't use dummies (we did), how our homes would not be filled with music-emitting plastic horrors (they are), how we would grow vegetables or visit art galleries or write novels during our maternity leaves (we did not) and how our children would play with one thing at a time, and then put it away (this has never happened to anyone, anywhere).

When the babies came, a frenzy of electronic messages pierced the endless nights. We fed and rocked and hushed and changed and sent up our panic and our bewilderment like flares, waiting for the message that would say, yes, this happened to their cousin and it was a sleep regression, it was teething, it was colic and – crucially – it passed. It was a lifeline in those early weeks to have the means to confer at midnight – I felt extremely lucky to live in our connected age, and can't imagine how lonely it must have been for generations before. We had dropped out of what I had previously considered our 'real lives', without a parachute and into strange new territory, together. There were days when getting to a baby group with milky vomit in only half my hair, wearing clothes that were indisputably daywear, having gulped a coffee that had only been microwaved twice, seemed an achievement akin to climbing a medium-sized mountain, and they *got it*. I recognise every one of the women in Polly Clark's poem 'Baby Group'. We congratulated each other on three-hour bursts of sleep, on spooning the tiniest dribble of pear into a reluctant mouth, on cutting the heart-stoppingly tiny nails.

There were other women, too, whose paths crossed mine only briefly, but who threw me a well-timed life raft. There was someone who wrote an article I read at three o'clock one morning about it being okay not to love everything about what Kathleen Jamie calls 'the first sweet-wild weeks'. There was a woman on the bus who, without me asking, efficiently packed up my buggy as I struggled to calm a squalling, kicking baby. In fact, I am eternally grateful to all the women on public transport who said the right thing, and *never*: 'Oh,' – sucking teeth disapprovingly – 'she's hungry.' I try to be among their number now.

I once attempted a Pilates class, during which the other babies reclined, cooing contentedly as their mothers did clever things to their cores. Only two, one of which was mine, refused to get with this peaceful programme, embarking on increasingly dramatic disruptive strategies. The other woman – a stranger –

and I gave up and fled in mortification, mollified the babies with a trip to the swings and stole a cackling afternoon in a pub garden that did me more good than anything else that year. Including the Pilates.

Nursery and school brought new pleasures – for them, messy play; for us, less messy play – but they have also ushered in an age of labyrinthine bureaucracy I couldn't possibly have navigated without hacks passed on from other mothers. These new friends provide playdates and dinner dates, holiday club pointers, emergency travel cots and sanity-saving audiobooks for long journeys. They have done the big things – scooping up the kids when my train is delayed – and the small but necessary ones – offering heartfelt condolences that school have sent home a recorder for the holidays.

Friends with older children have been a wellspring of comfort, emergency quiche deliveries, second-hand clothing and wisdom. (I made formal apologies to them for every time I had bemoaned how tired I was in my child-free days, which they graciously accepted. They are classy women.) I have never stopped turning to them for reassurance, tips and, occasionally, the freedom to vent about a particularly grisly school run. They are cheerleaders and counsellors. I could not be without them.

For every woman I met on the streets of Liz Berry's Republic of Motherhood who sympathised about an up-the-back poo, who shot me a look of amused solidarity while I negotiated with a toddler howling on the pavement because 'a dog left', who gave me socks for my baby's hands when I had come out in the cold without mittens: thank you. For everyone who admitted – in person or online – that they lost their temper, that they hadn't technically got dressed today, that their kids ate toasties every night this week, or that they didn't actually enjoy crafting: thank you. To the mothers and mothers-in-law, the sisters and friends, and the strangers who are up for an impromptu pub garden afternoon: here's to you. Here's to us.

Baby Group

Save me from my loneliness,
lady of the scar,

lady of the birth trauma
and the absent husband.

Distract me in the rain,
lady of the Asda fairy cake,

vacantly sipping as angels
circle in babywalkers.

And you, lady of perfection,
Boudica of cashmere

whose baby's shoes are shiny,
whose ribbons reek of adoration,

though we may never say more
than *hello, isn't she lovely!*

I am glad you exist.
You appear on a grey morning

right on time, smart as a sail
on bewildered waters.

Polly Clark

Daystar

She wanted a little room for thinking:
but she saw diapers steaming on the line,
a doll slumped behind the door.

So she lugged a chair behind the garage
to sit out the children's naps.

Sometimes there were things to watch –
the pinched armor of a vanished cricket,
a floating maple leaf. Other days
she stared until she was assured
when she closed her eyes
she'd see only her own vivid blood.

She had an hour, at best, before Liza appeared
pouting from the top of the stairs.
And just *what* was mother doing
out back with the field mice? Why,

building a palace. Later
that night when Thomas rolled over and
lurched into her, she would open her eyes
and think of the place that was hers
for an hour – where
she was nothing,
pure nothing, in the middle of the day.

Rita Dove

First Words

(for Ava)

Her fingers scrabble at glass,
over floorboards, table legs and chairs
to catch the word that runs away from her,
sifted through leaves, snatched up on a breeze,
stolen by clouds, returned.

Propelled on bottom, elbows, knees,
with silent determination, she follows it
and only when it spills out of her hand,
whispers, like someone in a church
or library, *sunshine*.

She knows the moon even when
it is nothing more than a curl on blue,
or half an ear listening for the next star.
Even the disc of milk in a bowl is *moon*.
She says the word and drinks it in.

Imtiaz Dharker

The View

So much of this is cowpoke work,
so much of this is gates and getting
through them – there could be a mountain
rearing above us, there could be a city
hung above the cloudline and still
I'd be keeping my eyes on your footprints,
still I'd be steering this flock home.

Do you think there is a mountain,
my darling, my poppet, stooped there
on your stick like the village elder?
Is it upside down in the depths
of that puddle? I shall flop down
beside you, straight-legged and muddy,
stir up a sunset in the altering oil.

Kate Clanchy

Extract from **Mama**

When mama sings *Ba ba black sheep*,
the stars seem to shine through her voice
so everything has to be still,
and when she has finished singing
her song goes up off the earth,
higher and higher …
till it is only as big as a tiny silver bird
with nothing but moonlight around it.

Lola Ridge

Light the Fire

Light the fire when night is near,
A little flame to span the night.
He will not feel the winds of fear
In the curved glades of firelight.

And sing smoothly if you sing,
Lest he should hear between the stresses
The insensible cold rain falling
In unpeopled wildernesses.

With your song and vaulted light
Build his brittle starless ark.
With a curtain on the night
Overthrow the wild and dark.

E. J. Scovell

For My Daughter

And later, when she asks, I'll say
some parts of it were beautiful –
how in their brightness
and sudden opening
the faces of the neighbours
began to look like flowers.
I'll tell her how we began
to look back at photos
of our younger selves
with our arms around a stranger
or leaning on the shoulders
of friends, and saw that touch
had always been a kind of holiness,
a type of worship we were promised.
I'll tell her that in some ways
our days shrunk to nothing,
being both as long as a year
and as quick as the turning of a page.
I'll tell her how she learned to crawl
in those days, in those times
when we could not leave,
when bodies were carried
from homes and were not counted,

that she began to say her first word
while death waited in the streets,
that though I was afraid,
I never saw fear in her eyes.

Kim Moore

Sugar Beet

'Jiggle, jiggle, jiggle, jiggle, tickle, tickle, tickle, tickle,
little sack of sugar I could eat you up'

– WOODY GUTHRIE

Pretending to eat cake
I sit you on the table just to look in your eyes
rub my nose with your nose kiss your toes
sticky hands on my lips and chin and we are lost
in a cloud of sweet flour.
In a cloud of sweet flour
we are lost, sticky hands on my lips and chin and
kiss your toes, rub my nose with your nose
just to look in your eyes, I sit you on the table
pretending to eat cake.

Rachel Bower

The Weighing of the Heart

What does the heart weigh?
More than the pull of your small
hand on mine? More than your head's
light heaviness on my shoulder?

Under the tender pressure of sleep
my old wool jacket becomes
your memory of consolation, comfort,
that ancient sweetness of love and tweed.

Remembering this, watching you,
I lose my place entirely, not knowing
whose the head, whose the sleeve,
whose the big hand and whose the small.

The Ancients measured a good heart
against the slightest puff of down,
in the gleam and glitter of delicate scales.
Like Thoth, we watch and wait.

What does the heart weigh?
Less than your head's tiny burden,
for lighter than a feather is love
and this the Egyptians knew.

Maura Dooley

The Visitor

Does no dishes, dribbles sauce
across the floor. Is more dragon
than spaniel, more flammable
than fluid. Is the loosening
in the knit of me, the mixed-fruit
marmalade in the kitchen of me.
Wakes my disco and inner hibiscus,
the Hector in the ever-mess of my Troy.
All wet mattress to my analysis,
he's stayed the loudest and longest
of any houseguest, is calling now
as I write this, tiny B who brings the joy.

Idra Novey

Ellen Learning to Walk

My beautiful trembler! how wildly she shrinks!
   And how wistful she looks while she lingers!
Papa is extremely uncivil, she thinks, –
   She but pleaded for one of his fingers!

What eloquent pleading! the hand reaching out,
   As if doubting so strange a refusal;
While her blue eyes say plainly, 'What is he about
   That he does not assist me as usual?'

Come on, my pet Ellen! we won't let you slip, –
   Unclasp those soft arms from his knee, love;
I see a faint smile round that exquisite lip,
   A smile half reproach and half glee, love.

So! that's my brave baby! one foot falters forward,
   Half doubtful the other steals by it!
What, shrinking again! why, you shy little coward!
   'Twon't kill you to walk a bit! – try it!

There! steady, my darling! huzza! I have caught her!
   I clasp her, caress'd and caressing!
And she hides her bright face, as if what we had taught her
   Were something to blush for – the blessing!

Now back again! Bravo! that shout of delight,
How it thrills to the hearts that adore her!
Joy, joy for her mother! and blest be the night,
When her little light feet first upbore her!

Frances Sargent Osgood

Reading to You

I've had some beautiful nights in my life –
sleepovers sneaking downstairs to the fridge
tiptoes with stomachs of bubbling giggles
and wrappers of Snickers and Magnums and dribbles

Some beautiful nights in my life –
on clifftops in sand dunes
on beaches with rave tunes and full moons and new friends
and neon and old scents and crap tents and butt ends
from haze-making grasses and pipes

I've had some beautiful nights in my life –
in beds and on couches
on Sundays just lounging
with comfort and calmness
and arms wrapped around me
and popcorn sounds drowning out
crunching through films
that flash me ideas
till my brain bursts
excitedly hatching up plans

I've had some beautiful nights
in my life

but sitting here
as the night falls
reading to you
as you point to the cow
and I attempt at a moo
and you laugh
and I do it again just for you
and the rain's pouring down
and the sound makes you calm

and your eyelids start sinking
and you battle them not to –
moulded into my arms
and that warm patch of skin
that spreads from your cheek
through your baby-wise grin
and I read to you softly
as your adrenalin gives
and I watch as you sink past that magical gate
turn-point between falling asleep from awake

Of all my nights and the stars I've walked through
Of all of the nights and the parties I've been to
I've had no greater night-times than reading to you
till you sleep
open-mouthed
ear on my arm
heart to my heart
with a laugh

as you drift into dreams
and I finish the book
though I know
you're already asleep

I stare at your face
in the still, silent room

The best nights of my life
have been reading to you.

Hollie McNish

To a Child

The leaves talked in the twilight, dear;
    Hearken the tale they told:
How in some far-off place and year,
    Before the world grew old,

I was a dreaming forest tree,
    You were a wild, sweet bird
Who sheltered at the heart of me
    Because the north wind stirred;

How, when the chiding gale was still,
    When peace fell soft on fear,
You stayed one golden hour to fill
    My dream with singing, dear.

To-night the self-same songs are sung
    The first green forest heard;
My heart and the gray world grow young –
    To shelter you, my bird.

Sophie Jewett

Portrait of Our Daughters

Like baby elephants, their ears and tails
are distinctive; witness their naked rumps
on the June lawn as they sport with water to cool down.
Their happiness too is elephantine – they sing
silly songs, snorkel and spout fountains,
then hurl themselves about on the trampoline
to get dry. We are nothing to them till they fight –
then there is barging and squeaking and they need us
to intervene. The cause, of course, is bewildering.
But finally they're assimilated back,
a herd unto themselves, kicking up the grass,
their strange, endangered joy trumpeted
for miles as they streak across the garden,
our crazy girls, our glorious, stampeding calves.

Fiona Benson

Mothers

(for J.B.)

Oh mother,
here in your lap,
as good as a bowlful of clouds,
I your greedy child
am given your breast,
the sea wrapped in skin,
and your arms,
roots covered with moss
and with new shoots sticking out
to tickle the laugh out of me.
Yes, I am wedded to my teddy
but he has the smell of you
as well as the smell of me.
Your necklace that I finger
is all angel eyes.
Your rings that sparkle
are like the moon on the pond.
Your legs that bounce me up and down,
your dear nylon-covered legs,
are the horses I will ride
into eternity.

Oh mother,
after this lap of childhood
I will never go forth
into the big people's world
as an alien,
a fabrication,
or falter
when someone else
is as empty as a shoe.

Anne Sexton

To the Breasts When It's Over –

You two heave heavies, glory rockers
right-on drop gold rum bumpers.

Didn't you divine & dine, feed &
fortify – you heaven-ed helpers, plenty

planters, mystifiers mag-fucking-nificent
the fact you fed for five years & now.

You make me mourn & moan, make
merry w/ *it's over*. Sure the baby

still needing nighttime nursing, you
dwindle to dribble. Infant to toddler

god (damn) soon enough these girls
will be *those girls* as you watch them

walkrunjumpdanceplaypunksneakdive
away from you. But you won't forget

there was a time when all their hunger
was quenched. By you.

Ellen Hagan

Where Are You?

It is entirely understandable that midwives and health visitors, faced with a continual procession of dazed and befuddled new mothers, resort to addressing us all by the generic term 'mum' – but it can be an eerie experience when that identity is still so fresh and raw. We knew, once, who we were, but it takes time for the knowledge of this new role to seep into our fibres. Whatever else you are, *you're always this*. So … where do you find the woman you remember being, as you blink, shipwrecked, on the shore of this new world?

I had been the child-free comrade on a night out, urging another glass because, 'You're off duty!' I had no concept of the night offices the newish mother would be

called to perform – what Liz Berry calls 'the owl shift …
Feedingcleaninglovingfeeding' – as I snored later. I just
wanted my friend back. When it was my turn and the fog
of the early weeks had begun to lift, I felt the same about
myself, wanting the old me back, too. The first time I
walked somewhere without pushing a pram, I thought
I might topple over or float away. Was I walking weirdly?
What had I ever done with my arms? Could anyone tell
that part of me had been severed?

My husband and I attempted an anniversary dinner
when my elder daughter was three months old. We had
learned to temper our ambitions. Our plans involved
no white table linen or obsequious waiters, just a
takeaway and the television. We took turns to eat curry
alone while the other, in the bedroom, frantically rocked
and shhhh-ed and patted to the deafening roar of the
only white noise app that seemed to placate her, in a
vain attempt to get her off to sleep. A few months later,
when my daughter had at last consented to sleep in
the cot and evenings existed again, the time seemed an
unimaginable luxury, and all the more precious for it.
(I'd love to tell you we spent it tucking into candlelit
feasts, but as I recall our schedule was rather more curry-
and-television based than that.) The tender but relentless
work of those newborn days can be so overwhelming

that it's hard, sometimes, to remember to be kind to each other as well.

I wanted so much to love my body for what it had done. In her beautiful poem 'Ruins', Fiona Benson writes, 'amen I say to all of this', but it isn't always easy to give our bodies the awestruck praise they're due for pulling off this most magical of conjuring tricks. I still barely recognise parts of me, and for a long time my body felt anything but my own, despite being single occupancy again. I'd never really understood that there was more to childbearing than a swelling stomach. Having been hitherto both ignorant and incurious, I was deeply affronted by all the new information about gums and joints and hair and anxiety around trampolines. I try, though. When the doctor sewing me up after my emergency caesarean kept assuring me the incision was low enough for me to wear a bikini, I cheerfully reassured him that I hadn't forged my career as a swimwear model. I paid for my children with these scars, these aches, those deeply flattering trousers that no longer fitted … but the price, though steep, wasn't too high.

While writing this, I messaged friends to ask: What about motherhood made you feel lost? What made you feel you had found yourself again? (One answered almost too perfectly, firing off messages between bouts of child-wrangling: *Oh wow, I have a lot of thoughts. Kids though. Will write tonight.*) Some talked about missing feeling competent. We were plunged into a new role for which we were untrained – though there was an expectation quite missing from other careers that it would 'come naturally', and a peculiar shame when it didn't. The hours were punishing, with colleagues – managers, really – whose demands were frequently both unreasonable and violently communicated.

Baby-care is all-consuming. The past really can feel like another country and the you who skipped off for an impromptu evening out, or even just read a book on a train, can feel like a figure from ancient myth: Kate Clanchy's 'other woman'. If you work, whatever arrangements you make, it will be different. Despite a love of what I call planning, and my husband calls fretting bordering on the obsessive, I don't think I ever peered past the baby days. (School finishes at *what* time?)

But there comes a moment when you'll feel a tickle of her, that person you used to be, like the tingling in a limb that's gone to sleep when the blood inches back in. Barking with inappropriate laughter as my cat enthusiastically humped the startled midwife's cardigan, I caught a glimpse of myself behind 'mum' again. When I realised I had read a page and a half of my book while minding an almost-toddler and a 4-year-old, the tunnel widened. Whether it's giving a keynote speech or simply having a wee with the door shut, the person you used to be is still there, though her pleasures and even her profession will need to be slotted into discrete windows of time, at least for a while. (And if you want something done, ask a mother. There is no wild efficiency like that of the woman who knows she might have ten minutes or two hours of naptime left in which to achieve a day's worth of everything.) She is sea-changed but she will surface.

The Other Woman

I am running to meet her,
now, the girl who lives on her own,
who has in her hand the key to her own
hallway, her own bare polished stair, who
is clacking down it now, in kitten heels, swearing,
who is marching over envelopes marked with a single name,
who is late, can be late, sleep late, forget things,
who tonight has forgotten hat, gloves and
umbrella, and is running not caring
through the luminous rain.
What shall we say?

Shall I slip off
my coat and order cold wine
and watch myself sip it through
the long row of optics, arching my back
on the velvet banquette? And pick up the wit,
the moue of the mouth as we pass jokes like olives?
And say the right thing and stand up for my round,
tapping the bar with a rolled-up twenty,
tipsy, self-conscious, a girl,
a vessel of secrets, so
carefully held in?

Or down just one glass
and see stars and the whole
room go smeary, have nothing to say
and say all the same – apropos of nothing,
in the middle of everything – *You don't understand.*
What happens in birth is someone slips from your side,
    someone
full-sized. Will she yawn, get her bag, start tucking
her fags in when I get out his photo,
say *Look, look how he's grown,*
all by himself, he has grown
to the size of my life?

                                            Kate Clanchy

A Brief Return

As the time comes to step over the threshold
to a place unknown, to the other side,
where quite suddenly a small human
will depend on your body for life,
everyone (everyone!) will tell you
there is nothing like it, and it is true.
No prayer no prophecy
can prepare you for what's to come.
And when it does, in the days and weeks that follow,
these words I'm about to tell you will seem
like the cruel punchline of a stand-up routine.
But let me promise you, there will come a time
even though it feels as otherworldly
as a lost language cast in ancient hieroglyphs,
like a cold wind slapping you across the cheek
for daring to even imagine something so brazen.
But let me promise you, though it will be as fleeting
as the flash of a dead loved one's face on a passing
    stranger,
there will come an afternoon
where you find yourself once again,
on the on-seven-six bus
riding south along Waterloo Bridge
watching from the top deck as
the river cross-sects the traffic under you,

or you'll greet yourself like a long lost friend,
staring at Rows of Pret sandwiches
knowing you'll pick up
the posh cheddar and pickle baguette
but wondering if you'll be drawn
to the pointlessness
of the jambon beurre.
You will step into the mundanity
of headphones-in, oyster-out,
tap through tap through
bustle hustle kerfuffle and yet.
Something about the everydayness
of it will make you feel alive again,
yourself again, immense again.
You might realise there is no rush out there like the rush
of running for the bus
and making it.

Yes, you were not too long ago plucked out of real-life
and set on a space-bound travelator
where the air is so pure, the lightheadedness is
    permanent.
And yes another human that once lived in your body
now lives outside of it and still depends on your body.
But that travelator? It has a return path.
You will come back to the Earth
one day I promise you.
You will take a bite out of that
posh cheddar baguette, while you stomp down Farringdon
    Road

between meetings. And for just a split second,
swimming in the indistinct familiarity of it, will wonder
if it really happened.

Roshni Goyate

To My Mother

O thou whose care sustained my infant years,
And taught my prattling lip each note of love;
Whose soothing voice breathed comfort to my fears,
And round my brow hope's brightest garland wove;

To thee my lay is due, the simple song,
Which Nature gave me at life's opening day;
To thee these rude, these untaught strains belong,
Whose heart indulgent will not spurn my lay.

O say, amid this wilderness of life,
What bosom would have throbbed like thine for me?
Who would have smiled responsive? – who in grief,
Would e'er have felt, and feeling, grieved like thee?

Who would have guarded, with a falcon eye,
Each trembling footstep or each sport of fear?
Who would have marked my bosom bounding high,
And clasped me to her heart, with love's bright tear?

Who would have hung around my sleepless couch,
And fanned, with anxious hand, my burning brow?
Who would have fondly pressed my fevered lip,
In all the agony of love and woe?

None but a mother – none but one like thee,
Whose bloom has faded in the midnight watch;
Whose eye, for me, has lost its witchery,
Whose form has felt disease's mildew touch.

Yes, thou hast lighted me to health and life,
By the bright lustre of thy youthful bloom –
Yes, thou hast wept so oft o'er every grief,
That woe hath traced thy brow with marks of gloom.

O then, to thee, this rude and simple song,
Which breathes of thankfulness and love for thee,
To thee, my mother, shall this lay belong,
Whose life is spent in toil and care for me.

Lucretia Maria Davidson

What a Little Girl Had on Her Mind

What a little girl had on her mind was:
Why do the shoulders of other men's wives
give off so strong a smell like magnolia;
or like gardenias?
What is it,
that faint veil of mist,
over the shoulders of other men's wives?
She wanted to have one,
that wonderful thing
even the prettiest virgin cannot have.

The little girl grew up.
She became a wife and then a mother.
One day she suddenly realised;
the tenderness
that gathers over the shoulders of wives,
is only fatigue
from loving others day after day.

Ibaragi Noriko
trans. Kenneth Rexroth and Ikuko Atsumi

Maybe the Milky Way

My son fills the inner space between my arm and body.
We lay in wet grass in the heart of the White Mountains,

far from the glare of city lights. *Maybe it's the Milky Way.*
Orion's belt drifts in a hemisphere so crowded with stars

we cannot locate it. We laugh, finger fine clusters of
    yellow-white
to create spirographs in star fields, our empty hands
    outstretched

and hungry—for what? We do not know. Like a private tour
of a planetarium's dome, it is our night. We know the stars

are watching us, would cast our shadows into the next galaxy
if they could. They watch him as I watch him, light
    reflecting light,

his beauty too dangerous to touch or hold or explain.
The love for my son would incinerate us if I get too close.

Tonight our hands girdle the heavens as we write new
    names
for ourselves, wishing on stars that neither shoot nor fall,

dissolve into stardust, while the campfire smoulders
and the marshmallows, unattended, burn orange to black.

January Gill O'Neil

Cleft

Such small hands
the cannula pins you down
alien weight on a wrist
slipping its plastic tag.
Twice you've been under
travelling solo
to that place beyond strip-light
thin sheets, lab smell.
Voyager, pilot, your tiny craft
in orbit round yourself.

First time back
you're screaming, black and blue
and clamped tight shut;
we hardly notice
your face made new.
Second time
a frequent flier
you wake and smile
but will not sleep again for weeks
or so it feels.

Four years later
in feverish nights
you find my bed
and press against me
lip to lip
until we drift together
to the place each found alone
and dream again the dream
that binds us
like a stitch.

Rachel Playforth

On My Own Little Daughter, Four Years Old

Sweet lovely infant, innocently gay,
  With blooming face arrayed in peaceful smiles,
How light thy cheerful heart doth sportive play,
  Unconscious of all future cares and toils.

With what delight I've seen thy little feet
  Dancing with pleasure at my near approach!
Eager they ran my well-known form to meet,
  Secure of welcome, fearless of reproach.

Then happy hast thou prattled in mine ear
  Thy little anxious tales of pain or joy;
Thy fears lest faithful Tray thy frock should tear,
  Thy pride when ladies give the gilded toy.

How oft, when sad reflection dimmed mine eye,
  As memory recalled past scenes of woe,
Thy tender heart hath heaved the expressive sigh
  Of sympathy, for ills thou could'st not know.

Oft too in silence I've admired that face,
  Beaming with pity for a mother's grief,
Whilst in each anxious feature I could trace
  Compassion eager to afford relief.

E'en now methinks I hear that artless tongue,
      Lisping sweet sounds of comfort to mine ear:
'Oh! fret no more – your Fanny is not gone –
      She will not go – don't cry – your Fanny's here.'

If, ere her mind attains its full-grown strength,
      Thy will consigns me to an early tomb,
If in Thy sight my thread's near run its length,
      And called by Thee I cannot watch her bloom –

Oh heavenly Father, guard my infant child;
      Protect her steps through this wide scene of care;
Within her breast implant each virtue mild,
      And teach her all she ought to hope or fear.

Anonymous

Limbs

Afraid of the dark, they find their way
to my bed at night; one hot, one cold
and no rest for any of us.

Sleepless elbows and knees find my hip,
shin, and the tender bone under my eye,
my body remembering a knot of child
kneading my bladder, stealing my breath,
stamping footprints on my belly.

These growing limbs –
needing new shoes, longer pants, another haircut;
these limbs that cling to me like vines to the face of a house –
they are working themselves free.

Against the curtain of their still small breaths,
truth dawns – these limbs will outlast me.
Worse, first
they will stop walking themselves
to my bedside at night.

Mary Walker

Ruby, Aged 4½

She's a roulette wheel loaded against you
A sure-fire bet when you don't have the stake
A gun in the hands of a man with a grudge
Like a smudge of silver leaf on a blacksmith's neck

She's a giggle that turns into a manic episode
An intermittent broadband connection
A delivery between nine in the morning and six at night
Like a bus driver who waits when he sees you running

She's a garden wall with loose brickwork
A ninety minute wait for a cab on your birthday
A higher than expected energy bill
Like a footballer with a doctorate in theology

She's an argument with your boyfriend's brother
A cobra squatting in a meerkat's den
A hooded teen walking behind you at night
Like a coin without a date stamp

She's a bit of a laugh that ends up in court
A train that blasts past at your station
A flag at full mast when the queen is dead
Like the difference between a common puffball
and a death cap. Like being alive.

Degna Stone

For a Five-Year-Old

A snail is climbing up the window-sill
into your room, after a night of rain.
You call me in to see, and I explain
that it would be unkind to leave it there:
it might crawl to the floor; we must take care
that no one squashes it. You understand,
and carry it outside, with careful hand,
to eat a daffodil.

I see, then, that a kind of faith prevails:
your gentleness is moulded still by words
from me, who have trapped mice and shot wild birds,
from me, who drowned your kittens, who betrayed
your closest relatives, and who purveyed
the harshest kind of truth to many another.
But that is how things are: I am your mother,
and we are kind to snails.

Fleur Adcock

To Mr Wren, My Valentine Six-Year-Old

Since the good Bishop left his name,
And men and maids kept up his fame,
Since birds in honour of his day
Married and went no more astray,
No she could boast a Valentine
Lovely and innocent as mine:
He has such a charming face,
A form so faultless, such a grace,
That, with some wax or silken strings
Fasten but on a pair of wings,
Poets and painters would mistake
And him for very Cupid take.
Then he has wit at will, and can
Pose the wisest, learned'st man:
Artful as Cowper he can plead,
And he can bow with any reed.

Oh! whene'er you'll be as good
As, if you pleased and tried, you could;
All fretful, childish tears give o'er,
And love your book a little more;
Cheerful and still at dinner sit,
Renowned for manners as for wit;

And softly round the chamber creep,
When your grandpapa's asleep:
Where could be found a youth so fine,
As my charming Valentine?

Jane Holt

Poem for Melissa

My fair-haired child dancing in the dunes
hair be-ribboned, gold rings on your fingers
to you, yet only five or six years old,
I grant you all on this delicate earth.

The fledgling bird out of the nest
the iris seeding in the drain
the green crab walking neatly sideways:
they are yours to see, my daughter.

The ox would gambol with the wolf
the child would play with the serpent
the lion would lie down with the lamb
in the pasture world I would delicately grant.

The garden gates forever wide open
no flaming swords in hands of Cherubim
no need for a fig-leaf apron here
in the pristine world I would delicately give.

Oh white daughter here's your mother's word:
I will put in your hand the sun and the moon
I will stand my body between the millstones
in God's mills so you are not totally ground.

Nuala Ní Dhomhnaill
trans. Michael Hartnett

A Child's Sleep

I stood at the edge of my child's sleep
hearing her breathe;
although I could not enter there,
I could not leave.

Her sleep was a small wood,
perfumed with flowers;
dark, peaceful, sacred,
acred in hours.

And she was the spirit that lives
in the heart of such woods;
without time, without history,
wordlessly good.

I spoke her name, a pebble dropped
in the still night,
and saw her stir, both open palms
cupping their soft light;

then went to the window. The greater dark
outside the room
gazed back, maternal, wise,
with its face of moon.

Carol Ann Duffy

Little Children

Politically they're puritans.
They gasp at nudity like it's 1912.
They're shocked by minor offences
such as chip stealing. 98% possess zero faith
in the concept of rehabilitation for adults.
As far as little children are concerned
forgivable mistakes occur before sixteen,
after that you're on your own. Their stance
against marital infidelity is Victorian and their
position on divorce aligns with the Vatican City.
Nuance is irrelevant to the infant moralist.
They sit in plastic umpire chairs at the dinner table
shouting out unintelligible scores. They're violent.
They'll head-bang a breast or stuff a sticky hand
up a skirt then just amble away
like raging misogynists. They won't even allow
their mothers to bring home a sexy stranger
on a Friday night. They disapprove of drugs
like Tory neighbours. Their standpoint on drunkenness
is predictably brutal, especially for women.
It's like the sixties never happened. They believe
every adult should be locked into a sexless yet eternal
marriage, never slip up or forget
even a lunchbox, and be completely transparent
and open to feedback 24/7. They're hypocrites.

They spy on you in the toilet. Parents aren't permitted
even the smallest private perversion yet a child
can secretly urinate in a drawer for three weeks
until the smell warrants investigation.
Their relentless indignation! Their fascist vision
of the perfect family! Little children are like
the tsarist autocracy of pre-revolution Russia.
Their soft hands have never known work.
Their reign is unearned.
On behalf of my younger self I apologise
to my parents for the simplistic, ill-informed
and ignorant questions I hurled concerning
their romantic and sexual life choices.
How could you do that to dad?
How could you do that to mum?
I was operating under a false consciousness,
responding to an imagined society governed
by laws I'd gleaned from picture books
about tigers coming to tea. I had no right.
No credibility. Imagine bellowing criticism
from the stalls after seeing two minutes of a play!
Imagine expecting universal loyalty whilst flinging
spaghetti hoops at the wall! Imagine having such
confidence in your innate philosophy of love!

We kneel to tie the laces of their unfeasibly tiny shoes.

Caroline Bird

The worlds

My mum made us many worlds
overlapping in bright circles,
and made us the shape-shifting shoes
to stride into them.

She made England
and she made Australians,
mouths filled with eucalyptus phrases;

she made shop-owners,
plying our biscuits and lemonade
to ramblers in our lane

and she made ramblers,
free from the hard charm of destination.

She made an artist's daughters,
story-hearers, and selective believers.
She made tree-dwellers,
trend-leavers and fancy-dress-wearers,

irregular pegs. She made the round holes
shimmy, she made silly,
she made kindness, she made calm.

My mum makes us the world
as wide as the world
and as small as the circle of her arms.

Rachel Piercey

Ode on the Whole Duty of Parents

The spirits of children are remote and wise,
They must go free
Like fishes in the sea
Or starlings in the skies,
Whilst you remain
The shore where casually they come again.
But when there falls the stalking shade of fear,
You must be suddenly near,
You, the unstable, must become a tree
In whose unending heights of flowering green
Hangs every fruit that grows, with silver bells;
Where heart-distracting magic birds are seen
And all the things a fairy-story tells;
Though still you should possess
Roots that go deep in ordinary earth,
And strong consoling bark
To love and to caress.

Last, when at dark
Safe on the pillow lies an up-gazing head
And drinking holy eyes
Are fixed on you,
When, from behind them, questions come to birth
Insistently,
On all the things that you have ever said
Of suns and snakes and parallelograms and flies,

And whether these are true,
Then for a while you'll need to be no more
That sheltering shore
Or legendary tree in safety spread,
No, then you must put on
The robes of Solomon,
Or simply be
Sir Isaac Newton sitting on the bed

Frances Cornford

Isaac Plays the Part of the Sun

My son dances in orange and gold
carried high by a stronger boy
and there's such joy
that my heart swells
until my sternum splits
crack, crack
with the beauty of it
each leap
each hold
each lift.

Helen Cadbury

The Temple of the Wood Lavender

A perfum'd sprig of lavender
You gave, dear child, to me;
It grew, you said, by the red rose bed,
And under the jessamine tree.

'Twas sweet, ay, sweet from many things;
But (sweeter than all) with scent
Of long past years and laughter and tears
It to me was redolent.

Lady Caroline Blanche Elizabeth Lindsay

Human Affection

Mother, I love you so.
Said the child, I love you more than I know.
She laid her head on her mother's arm,
And the love between them kept them warm.

Stevie Smith

Mother

The water of her womb, your first home.
The body she pulled apart to welcome you to the world.
The spirit in you she helped grow with all she knew.
The heart that she gave you when yours fell apart.
You are her soft miracle.
So she gave you her eyes to see the best in the worst.
You carry your mother in your eyes.
Make her proud of all she watches you do.

Nikita Gill

Making a Fist

For the first time, on the road north of Tampico,
I felt the life sliding out of me,
a drum in the desert, harder and harder to hear.
I was seven, I lay in the car
watching palm trees swirl a sickening pattern past the glass.
My stomach was a melon split wide inside my skin.

'How do you know if you are going to die?'
I begged my mother.
We had been traveling for days.
With strange confidence she answered,
'When you can no longer make a fist.'

Years later I smile to think of that journey,
the borders we must cross separately,
stamped with our unanswerable woes.
I who did not die, who am still living,
still lying in the backseat behind all my questions,
clenching and opening one small hand.

Naomi Shihab Nye

Vixen

motherhood peels me bare
like a willow wand
some small child scrapes in the road
or throws in the pond

motherhood aches me pale
I bleed with my child's wound
and hurt with his friend's unfriendliness
I climb with his bruise

motherhood grows me brave
now no mere woman nor wife
the vixen who fights for her cubs
will fight for her life

Glenda Beagan

I know you only invited me in for a coffee, but

I have eaten your house
Our children were playing inside

I say playing – actually your child
Was ignoring my child in a meanish, unkind sort of a way

Anyway I have eaten them now
So it is irrelevant that your child is not a kind person

I ate your 4×4 too
Even though I cannot drive

I am better than M. Mangetout –
Rather than, say, getting to work on a hubcap

I just swallow these things whole.
How will you drive the streets of Muswell Hill now?

I am breathing fire and a bit too busy to help.

Natalie Shaw

To My First Love, My Mother

Sonnets are full of love, and this my tome
Has many sonnets: so here now shall be
One sonnet more, a love sonnet, from me
To her whose heart is my heart's quiet home,
To my first Love, my Mother, on whose knee
I learnt love-lore that is not troublesome;
Whose service is my special dignity,
And she my lodestar while I go and come.
And so because you love me, and because
I love you, Mother, I have woven a wreath
Of rhymes wherewith to crown your honoured name:
In you not fourscore years can dim the flame
Of love, whose blessed glow transcends the laws
Of time and change and mortal life and death.

Christina Rossetti

Joseph Sleeps,

his eyelids like a moth's fringed wings.
Arms flail against the Ninja Turtle sheet
and suddenly-long legs
race time.

Awake, he's a water-leak detector, a recycling ranger
who bans Styrofoam and asks for beeswax
crayons, a renewable resource.
He wants to adopt the Missouri river,
write the president
to make factories stop polluting.

They're old friends, he and George Bush.
He writes and scolds
the president, every month or so,
about the bombing the children of Iraq
(he made his own sign to carry in protest),
about the plight of the California condor and northern
    gray wolf,
about more shelters and aid for the homeless.
The lion-shaped bulletin board in his room
is covered with pictures and letters from George,
who must be nice,
even if he is a slow learner.

Joseph is a mystery fan, owns 54 Nancy Drews.
Nancy's his friend, along with Jo, Meg, and Amy
and poor Beth, of course, whom he still mourns.
He also reads of knights and wizards, superheroes,
and how to win at Nintendo.

The cats and houseplants are his to feed and water
and the sunflower blooming in the driveway's border
of weeds. He drew our backyard to scale,
using map symbols, sent off to have it declared
an official wildlife refuge, left a good-night
note on my pillow, written in Egyptian hieroglyphs.

In my life, I have done one good thing.

Linda Rodriguez

Little Girl, My String Bean, My Lovely Woman

My daughter, at eleven
(almost twelve), is like a garden.

Oh, darling! Born in that sweet birthday suit
and having owned it and known it for so long,
now you must watch high noon enter –
noon, that ghost hour.
Oh, funny little girl – this one under a blueberry sky,
this one! How can I say that I've known
just what you know and just where you are?

It's not a strange place, this odd home
where your face sits in my hand
so full of distance,
so full of its immediate fever.
The summer has seized you,
as when, last month in Amalfi, I saw
lemons as large as your desk-side globe –
that miniature map of the world –
and I could mention, too,
the market stalls of mushrooms
and garlic buds all engorged.
Or I think even of the orchard next door,
where the berries are done
and the apples are beginning to swell.

And once, with our first backyard,
I remember I planted an acre of yellow beans
we couldn't eat.

Oh, little girl,
my string bean,
how do you grow?
You grow this way.
You are too many to eat.

I hear
as in a dream
the conversation of the old wives
speaking of *womanhood.*
I remember that I heard nothing myself.
I was alone.
I waited like a target.

Let high noon enter –
the hour of the ghosts.
Once the Romans believed
that noon was the ghost hour,
and I can believe it, too,
under that startling sun,
and someday they will come to you,
someday, men bare to the waist, young Romans
at noon where they belong,
with ladders and hammers
while no one sleeps.

But before they enter
I will have said,
Your bones are lovely,
and before their strange hands
there was always this hand that formed.

Oh, darling, let your body in,
let it tie you in,
in comfort.
What I want to say, Linda,
is that women are born twice.

If I could have watched you grow
as a magical mother might,
if I could have seen through my magical transparent belly,
there would have been such ripening within:
your embryo,
the seed taking on its own,
life clapping the bedpost,
bones from the pond,
thumbs and two mysterious eyes,
the awfully human head,
the heart jumping like a puppy,
the important lungs,
the becoming –
while it becomes!
as it does now,
a world of its own,
a delicate place.

I say hello
to such shakes and knockings and high jinks,
such music, such sprouts,
such dancing-mad-bears of music,
such necessary sugar,
such goings-on!

Oh, little girl,
my string bean,
how do you grow?
You grow this way.
You are too many to eat.

What I want to say, Linda,
is that there is nothing in your body that lies.
All that is new is telling the truth.
I'm here, that somebody else,
an old tree in the background.

Darling,
stand still at your door,
sure of yourself, a white stone, a good stone –
as exceptional as laughter
you will strike fire,
that new thing!

Anne Sexton

Milestones

There are poems here about every stage of motherhood –
from the first kicks, through the first words and staggering
steps, to the flight from the nest. I love the reminders they
give us that though the days are long – and they certainly
seem so when they're filled with tense negotiations about
pants and snacks – the years are short.

Some of these verses take me back: to that tentative
first pram-pushing, wincing at the joins in the pavement,
or the electric moment in which your baby makes eye
contact, perhaps gives a dignified but wobbly nod,
and actually *notices* you. I'd kill for an ounce of that
connection some mornings now that mine are older,
when I'm incoherently bellowing about brushing your

shoes and putting your teeth on for the umpteenth time. I love, though, that so many of these poems celebrate the miraculous, if sometimes exasperating *separateness*, of someone who was once a part of yourself. It is both a sweet pain and a liberation that they will be who they are. Christy Ducker describes her baby so beautifully as 'you and young and other'. 'What we began,' writes Anne Ridler, 'is now its own.'

I could never have predicted the sheer giddy buzz when the first animal noises were pronounced, or the exultation when I was finally addressed as 'Mummy'. (It came some time after 'Daddy' with my elder daughter, who waved away the question of my name for months with a slight puzzled frown, like a polite but amnesiac elderly aunt. I tried not to sulk about it. Obviously, I failed.) What could match the delighted thrill of the mastered clap, the point, the high five and the blown raspberry, or the profoundly serious inaugural performance of bobbin winding? We rhapsodised over the first picture by my younger daughter that looked unmistakably like a face, heralding a year's worth of artistic endeavours boasting peculiarly expressive potato people ('You have three legs, like a spider, Mummy. And you're sad.') We whooped when – at last – both were bombing about on bikes.

Some milestones are almost universal: the scrap of child swamped by a stiff school uniform, smiling uncertainly on the doorstep, or the ceremonial retirement of the buggy. But we each cherish our own private moments of transition, too. I remember exchanging awed glances with my husband the first time we heard our elder daughter take herself to the bathroom independently at night – not an occasion there's a greetings card range for – and a friend still speaks with pleasure-glazed eyes about the weekend morning when she first read the newspaper in peace. Every family has their own waymarkers on this road.

There are poems here I love for their clear-eyed and hilariously credible portraits of children, from Degna Stone's 4-and-a-half-year-old – 'She's a bit of a laugh that ends up in court' – to Caroline Bird's tiny tyrants: 'Imagine expecting universal loyalty whilst flinging / spaghetti hoops at the wall!' These poems paint real kids, in all their eccentric, grubby pomp. I recognise in these pages women whose children have, like my own strong-minded younger daughter, devoted many hours to howling on floors about injustices including – but not limited to – being presented with a less fancy spoon, the suggestion of a jumper or the offer to peel a tangerine.

I love, too, that there are poems here that let me imagine, for a moment, times to come. I've often thought that parenting would be enormously improved by being able to switch your children's ages once a month. On that day, instead of being bombarded from 5am by incessant questions – 'Where is that bird going? Why is that a lorry? What is green?' – the frazzled parent could enjoy a restful day of communication only in grunts from their now teenaged son. Or the mother of a pre-teen sophisticate, capable of cosying up through *Little Women* with a hot chocolate, could for that day wrangle a chubby, guffawing, endearing but exhausting toddler who needs a new activity established every seven minutes from sunrise. We would return to the frontline appreciative and refreshed after such a glimpse forward or backwards. When I get half a second to hear myself think, I'll start a petition.

Rachel Hadas speaks of the first semi-independent walks to school, the parent's heart stretching 'elastic in its love and fear' after a striding son. And there is rugby, and nights out, fashionable clothes and gap years and the long, slow letting go, and these poems are as brave and beautiful and devastating as any set on the labour ward. I asked my mother about when I left home – I don't remember glancing backwards even for an instant – and she wrote to me, with perfect, agonising words, that the waves of desolation felt like 'homesickness in reverse'. We lose ourselves a little in our children, but we live in them, too.

What My Kids Will Write about Me in Their Future Tell-All Book

They will say that no was my favourite word,
More than stop, or eat, or love.

That some mornings, I'd rather stay in bed,
laptop on lap, instead of making breakfast,
that I'd rather write than speak.

They will say they have seen me naked.
Front side, back side – none of which
were my good side.

They will say I breastfed too long.

In the tell-all book my kids will write
they'll tell how I let them wrinkle like raisins
in the bathtub so I could watch Big Papi at the plate.

They'll talk about how I threw out their artwork,
the watercolors and turkey hands,
when I thought they weren't looking
and when I knew they were.

They'll say that my voice was a slow torture,
that my singing caused them permanent hearing loss.

In the tell-all book my kids will write
as surely as I am writing this, they will say
I cut them off mid-sentence just because I could.

They'll tell you how I got down on my knees,
growling my low, guttural disapproval,
how I grabbed their ears, pinched the backs of their arms
yet they never quite knew who was sadder for it.

They'll quote me saying, *I cry in the shower –
it's the only safe place I can go.*
They will say she was 'our sweetest disaster.'

They will say I loved them so much it hurt.

January Gill O'Neil

The Red Hat

It started before Christmas. Now our son
Officially walks to school alone.
Semi-alone, it's accurate to say:
I or his father track him on the way.
He walks up on the east side of West End,
we on the west side. Glances can extend
(and do) across the street; not eye contact.
Already ties are feeling and not fact.
Straus Park is where these parallel paths part;
he goes alone from there. The watcher's heart
stretches, elastic in its love and fear,
toward him as we see him disappear,
striding briskly. Where two weeks ago,
holding a hand, he'd dawdle, dreamy, slow,
he now is hustled forward by the pull
of something far more powerful than school.
The mornings we turn back to are no more
than forty minutes longer than before,
but they feel vastly different – flimsy, strange,
wavering in the eddies of this change,
empty, unanchored, perilously light
since the red hat vanished from our sight.

Rachel Hadas

Even as I Hold You

Even as I hold you
I think of you as someone gone
far, far away. Your eyes the color
of pennies in a bowl of dark honey
bringing sweet light to someone else
your black hair slipping through my fingers
is the flash of your head going
around a corner
your smile, breaking before me,
the flippant last turn
of a revolving door,
emptying you out, changed,
away from me.

Even as I hold you
I am letting you go.

Alice Walker

Extract from **In Reference to Her Children, 23rd June 1659**

Great was my pain when I you bred,
Great was my care, when I you fed,
Long did I keep you soft and warm,
And with my wings kept off all harm.
My cares are more, and fears, than ever,
My throbs such now as 'fore were never.
Alas, my birds, you wisdom want
Of perils you are ignorant.
Oft times in grass, on trees, in flight,
Sore accidents on you may light.
O to your safety have an eye,
So happy may you live and die.
Mean while, my days in tunes I'll spend
Till my weak lays with me shall end.
In shady woods I'll sit and sing
And things that past, to mind I'll bring.

Anne Bradstreet

Huge Blue

(for Jack)

You were three when we moved north,
near the sea. That first time
you took one look, twisted off your clothes
till, bare as the day you were born,

you made off: I had to sprint,
scoop you up just as you threw the whole of you
into its huge blue – or you might be swimming still,
half way to Murmansk, that port you always dreamed of
    seeing:

I once flew, about your age:
strong arms held me hard,
hauled me down so my salted eyelashes
stuck together, sucked blue dark:

I didn't know how to remember
until you opened your arms that day,
sure that the world would hold you
and it did: grown now, and half a world away,

I hope your huge blue
is beautiful with stars
as you leap, eyes wide open,
no ghost of me on your back.

Pippa Little

In October in the Kitchen
I Listen to My Son

explain he needs a shooting game. I don't get
the beauty of open world, roaming freely
city to country, joint in hand, cops at your back;
I don't understand how great speed feels. Right.

Out the kitchen window the world we made
only 10,000 years old: vines, trees, morning mists
just like the Keats poem. So easy to miss even small
wonder: spiders, squirrels in lettuce boxes, fox.

I am that slow and would like to get slower still.
One lifetime is not really enough, I tell him. No.
Don't go into the cave, my son, the piper's calling.
Here on the other side, I'll be waiting.

Catherine Temma Davidson

How Can That Be My Baby?

How can that be my baby? How can that be my son?
Standing on a rugger field, no more than six feet one
Steam is rising from him, his legs are streaked with blood
And he wears a yellow mouthguard in a face that's black
   with mud.

How can that be my baby? How can he look like that?
I used to sit him on my knee and read him Postman Pat
Those little ears with cotton buds I kept in perfect shape
But now they're big and purple, they're fastened back
   with tape.

How can that be my baby? How did he reach that size?
What happened to his wellies with the little froggy eyes?
His shirt is on one shoulder but it's hanging off the other
And the little baffled person at his feet is me: his mother.

Pam Ayres

Fenrir

He slips in before dawn, a shadow running with wolves.
That thatch of hair, once slicked wet over the fontanelle,
is hidden, hooded. Grey eyes, grown used to darkness,
catch and shine. I know the blood in his veins is mine.

Daylight. I watch him sleep, pale as death, then I retreat
over nests of underwear. Just before I close the door
on sour air, I gather up one huge shoe and feel again
the foot that hit my ribcage with its first fierce kick.

Helen Cadbury

Praise Song for My Mother

You were
water to me
deep and bold and fathoming

You were
moon's eye to me
pull and grained and mantling

You were
sunrise to me
rise and warm and streaming

You were
the fishes red gill to me
the flame tree's spread to me
the crab's leg/the fried plantain smell replenishing
   replenishing

Go to your wide futures, you said

Grace Nichols

Gap Year

(for Mateo)

I

I remember your Moses basket before you were born.
I'd stare at the fleecy white sheet for days, weeks,
willing you to arrive, hardly able to believe
I would ever have a real baby to put in the basket.

I'd feel the mound of my tight tub of a stomach,
and you moving there, foot against my heart,
elbow in my ribcage, turning, burping, awake, asleep.
One time I imagined I felt you laugh.

I'd play you Handel's Water Music or Emma Kirkby
singing Pergolesi. I'd talk to you, my close stranger,
call you Tumshie, ask when you were coming to meet me.
You arrived late, the very hot summer of eighty-eight.

You had passed the due date string of eights,
and were pulled out with forceps, blue, floury,
on the fourteenth of August on Sunday afternoon.
I took you home on Monday and lay you in your basket.

II

Now, I peek in your room and stare at your bed
hardly able to imagine you back in there sleeping,
Your handsome face – soft, open. Now you are eighteen,
six foot two, away, away in Costa Rica, Peru, Bolivia.

I follow your trails on my Times Atlas:
from the Caribbean side of Costa Rica to the Pacific,
the baby turtles to the massive leatherbacks.
Then on to Lima, to Cuzco. Your grandfather

rings: 'Have you considered altitude sickness,
Christ, he's sixteen thousand feet above sea level.'
Then to the lost city of the Incas, Macchu Picchu,
Where you take a photograph of yourself with the statue

of the original Tupac. You are wearing a Peruvian hat.
Yesterday in Puno before catching the bus for Copacabana,
you suddenly appear on a webcam and blow me a kiss,
you have a new haircut; your face is grainy, blurry.

Seeing you, shy, smiling, on the webcam reminds me
of the second scan at twenty weeks, how at that fuzzy
moment back then, you were lying cross-legged with
an index finger resting sophisticatedly on one cheek.

You started the Inca trail in Arctic conditions
and ended up in subtropical. Now you plan the Amazon
in Bolivia. Your grandfather rings again to say
'There's three warring factions in Bolivia, warn him

against it. He canny see everything. Tell him to come home.'
But you say all the travellers you meet rave about Bolivia.
You want to see the Salar de Uyuni,
the world's largest salt-flats, the Amazonian rainforest.

And now you are not coming home till four weeks after
your due date. After Bolivia, you plan to stay
with a friend's Auntie in Argentina.
Then – to Chile where you'll stay with friends of Diane's.

And maybe work for the Victor Jara Foundation.
I feel like a home-alone mother; all the lights
have gone out in the hall, and now I am
wearing your large black slippers, flip-flopping

into your empty bedroom, trying to imagine you
in your bed. I stare at the photos you send by messenger:
you on the top of the world, arms outstretched, eager.
Blue sky, white snow; you by Lake Tararhua, beaming.

My heart soars like the birds in your bright blue skies.
My love glows like the sunrise over the lost city.
I sing along to Ella Fitzgerald, A tisket A tasket.
I have a son out in the big wide world.

A flip and a skip ago, you were dreaming in your basket.

Jackie Kay

The First Shoes

The first shoes that you wore weren't even shoes
but socks printed with laces; then you crawled
and stumbled into blunt bright moccasins.
The first shoes that were worthy of the name,
odd little things so soft they flexed like gloves,
were stitched about with warnings: do not crush
or warp or twist such tiny, tender feet,
growing like mushrooms in the cradling dark.
Then other firsts stacked like a deck of cards:
wellies with reptile smiles, plastic glass slippers,
dance glitter with a daring inch-high heel,
pompoms and plush. Uncountable split sneakers,
hot asphalt scuffs, backs casual trodden-down
(lone rogues kicked off to trip us on the stairs.)
The first school shoes, the patent Mary Janes,
grown-up in photos under puddled socks,
give way at speed to boots in which to run,
to scramble up the vertical, to kick
holes in the world, and its enclosing walls.
Now, for the first time, you are at my heels;
now your demure black shoe fits my whole foot,
I realise how soon you'll walk away.

Imogen Russell Williams

To a Daughter Leaving Home

When I taught you
at eight to ride
a bicycle, loping along
beside you
as you wobbled away
on two round wheels,
my own mouth rounding
in surprise when you pulled
ahead down the curved
path of the park,
I kept waiting
for the thud
of your crash as I
sprinted to catch up,
while you grew
smaller, more breakable
with distance,
pumping, pumping
for your life, screaming
with laughter,
the hair flapping
behind you like a
handkerchief waving
goodbye.

Linda Pastan

Day to Celebrate You Leaving Home

(for Esther)

If I could padlock today to the Millennium Bridge
I'd lock the Thames saturated in grey,
the Shard blotted in mist,
St Paul's arching over a corner of the sky;

our discussion on the difference between art and craft
on the steps of the Turbine Hall
before we climbed to the Miró,
our laughter at the gouache
'Woman With Blonde Armpit Combing Her Hair
by the Light of the Stars'
in Room 7.

I'd lock our agreement that the quickest painting
in the National Portrait Gallery award exhibition
was the best, your choice of
black hardback notebooks, green rubber,
and clutch of bargain canvases in the shop
with its annual sale.

And you, sat at my feet in the coach station,
your hair tangled and tamed,
your navel jewel glinting
behind your black lacy top.

Chrissie Gittins

Advice for My Daughters

Don't believe the first things,
don't believe the last things,
believe what you see.

Don't sit too close to drains
or spend too long at a stove.
Always know where the exit is.

Don't store too much.
Know what to give away.
Hold as much as you can carry.

If you have children give them magic,
soft songs, a coin under a pillow,
but don't give them everything.

Sleep in good linen, enjoy the smell of lemon,
breathe deeply, dream deeply,
if you don't know what to do, do something.

Don't diet, or be a martyr.
Life is suffering, but you are lucky
so you might as well be happy.

Julia Darling

All the things you are not yet

(for Tess)

Tonight there's a crowd in my head:
all the things you are not yet.
You are words without paper, pages
sighing in summer forests, gardens
where builders stub out their rubble
and plastic oozes its sweat.
All the things you are, you are not yet.

Not yet the lonely window in midwinter
with the whine of tea on an empty stomach,
not yet the heating you can't afford and must wait for,
tamping a coin in on each hour.
Not the gorgeous shush of restaurant doors
and their interiors, always so much smaller.
Not the smell of the newsprint, the blur
on your fingertips – your fame. Not yet

the love you will have for Winter Pearmains
and Chanel No 5 – and then your being unable
to buy both washing-machine and computer
when your baby's due to be born,
and my voice saying, 'I'll get you one'
and you frowning, frowning
at walls and surfaces which are not mine –
all this, not yet. Give me your hand,

that small one without a mark of work on it,
the one that's strange to the washing-up bowl
and doesn't know Fairy Liquid from whiskey.
Not yet the moment of your arrival in taxis
at daring destinations, or your being alone at stations
with the skirts of your fashionable clothes flapping
and no money for the telephone.

Not yet the moment when I can give you nothing
so well-folded it fits in an envelope –
a dull letter you won't reread.
Not yet the moment of your assimilation
in that river flowing westward: rivers of clothes,
of dreams, an accent unlike my own
saying to someone I don't know: *darling ...*

Helen Dunmore

XX

from

Mother and Daughter Sonnets

There's one I miss. A little questioning maid
That held my finger, trotting by my side,
And smiled out of her pleased eyes open wide,
Wondering and wiser at each word I said.
And I must help her frolics if she played,
And I must feel her trouble if she cried;
My lap was hers past right to be denied;
She did my bidding, but I more obeyed.

Dearer she is to-day, dearer and more;
Closer to me, since sister womanhoods meet;
Yet, like poor mothers some long while bereft,
I dwell on toward ways, quaint memories left,
I miss the approaching sound of pit-pat feet,
The eager baby voice outside my door.

Augusta Webster

XVI

from

Mother and Daughter Sonnets

She will not have it that my day wanes low,
Poor of the fire its drooping sun denies,
That on my brow the thin lines write good-byes
Which soon may be read plain for all to know,
Telling that I have done with youth's brave show;
Alas! and done with youth in heart and eyes,
With wonder and with far expectancies,
Save but to say 'I knew such long ago.'

She will not have it. Loverlike to me,
She with her happy gaze finds all that's best,
She sees this fair and that unfretted still,
And her own sunshine over all the rest:
So she half keeps me as she'd have me be,
And I forget to age, through her sweet will.

Augusta Webster

She describes herself like this

I still choose the window seat on buses,
trains and planes and though for now
all I can see is my own reflection
in the glass, in the fading light,
sometimes I can see beyond it.

I am a mother, a field   a house.
Without me, windows darken,
no-one else knows how to put on lights
just to bring the house to life.

I am each of the processes of laundry,
but most, the unfolding in winter
of sheets –   a sudden punch
of trapped summer on white linen – heat.

I have had many lovers
and I have been many times loved.
When I come I cry out,

and I am the sound of the wind in the trees

and I am the rain on the roof when in love,

or falling.

Deborah Alma

The Raincoat

When the doctor suggested surgery
and a brace for all my youngest years,
my parents scrambled to take me
to massage therapy, deep tissue work,
osteopathy, and soon my crooked spine
unspooled a bit, I could breathe again,
and move more in a body unclouded
by pain. My mom would tell me to sing
songs to her the whole forty-five minute
drive to Middle Two Rock Road and forty-
five minutes back from physical therapy.
She'd say, even my voice sounded unfettered
by my spine afterward. So I sang and sang,
because I thought she liked it. I never
asked her what she gave up to drive me,
or how her day was before this chore. Today,
at her age, I was driving myself home from yet
another spine appointment, singing along
to some maudlin but solid song on the radio,
and I saw a mom take her raincoat off
and give it to her young daughter when
a storm took over the afternoon. My god,
I thought, my whole life I've been under her
raincoat thinking it was somehow a marvel
that I never got wet.

Ada Limón

CREDITS

Trapeze would like to thank everyone at Orion who worked on the publication of *Night Feeds and Morning Songs* in the UK.

Editor
Sam Eades

Editorial Management
Jo Whitford
Charlie Panayiotou
Jane Hughes
Claire Boyle

Audio
Paul Stark
Amber Bates

Contracts
Anne Goddard
Paul Bulos
Jake Alderson

Design
Debbie Holmes
Joanna Ridley

Nick May
Clare Sivell
Helen Ewing
Rachel Lancaster

Finance
Jennifer Muchan
Jasdip Nandra
Ibukun Ademefun
Rabale Mustafa
Sue Baker
Tom Costello

Marketing
Jennifer Hope

Production
Claire Keep
Fiona McIntosh

Publicity
Alex Layt

Sales
Jennifer Wilson
Victoria Laws
Esther Waters
Lucy Brem
Frances Doyle
Ben Goddard
Georgina Cutler
Jack Hallam
Ellie Kyrke-Smith
Inês Figuiera
Barbara Ronan
Andrew Hally
Dominic Smith
Deborah Deyong
Lauren Buck
Maggy Park
Linda McGregor
Sinead White
Jemimah James

Rachel Jones
Jack Dennison
Nigel Andrews
Ian Williamson
Julia Benson
Declan Kyle
Robert Mackenzie
Imogen Clarke
Megan Smith
Charlotte Clay
Rebecca Cobbold

Operations
Jo Jacobs
Sharon Willis
Lisa Pryde

Rights
Susan Howe
Richard King
Krystyna Kujawinska
Jessica Purdue
Louise Henderson

ACKNOWLEDGEMENTS

First and foremost, I want to thank every poet – living and dead – who produced work that made me smile, cry and feel less alone while editing this book in lockdown with my children. You are all magicians. Thank you for allowing us to include your amazing poems.

A huge thank you to Sam Eades for offering me this longed-for opportunity – partly, I suspect, in sympathy for my tweets about my four-year-old's behaviour – and for her incredibly hard work in the same locked-down-without-childcare boat. Both she and Jo Whitford improved the book beyond measure every time they touched it. Enormous thanks also to my magnificent publicist Alex Layt and marketeer Jennifer Hope.

Thanks, always, to my mother for absolutely everything. This book is also dedicated in loving memory to Janet McLaughlin, my wonderful and much-missed mother-in-law.

And thank you to all the women who've done this mad thing, through mad and less mad times, with me. You are all incredible.

PERMISSIONS

The compiler and publisher would like to thank the following for permission to use their copyrighted material:

Adcock, Fleur: 'For a Five-Year-Old' from *Poems 1960–2000* (Bloodaxe Books, 2000). Copyright © Fleur Adcock. Reproduced by permission of the publisher; **Alma, Deborah:** 'She describes herself like this' from *Dirty Laundry* (Nine Arches Press, 2018). Copyright © Deborah Alma. Reproduced by permission of the publisher; **Ayres, Pam:** 'How Can That Be My Baby?'. Extract from 'How Can That Be My Baby' in *With These Hands* by Pam Ayres published by Ebury in 2021. © How Can That Be My Baby 2021. Reproduced by permission of Sheil Land Associates Ltd; **Ayuning Maharsi, Ikhda:** 'Bambino' from *Motherhood* (The Emma Press, 2014). Copyright © Ikhda Ayuning Maharsi. Reproduced by permission of the author; **Baer, Kate:** 'Young Mother' copyright © 2020 by Kate Baer. Reproduced by permission of the author; **Beagan, Glenda:** 'Vixen' from *Vixen* (Honno, 1996). Copyright © Glenda Beagan. Reproduced by permission of the author; **Bellamacina, Greta:** 'Never Letting Go' from *Smear* (Andrews McMeel, 2020). Copyright © Greta Bellamacina. Reproduced by permission of Conville and Walsh Ltd; **Benson, Fiona:** 'Portraits of Our Daughters' and 'Ruins'

Help us make the next generation of readers

We – both author and publisher – hope you enjoyed this book. We believe that you can become a reader at any time in your life, but we'd love your help to give the next generation a head start.

Did you know that 9 per cent of children don't have a book of their own in their home, rising to 13 per cent in disadvantaged families*? We'd like to try to change that by asking you to consider the role you could play in helping to build readers of the future.

We'd love you to think of sharing, borrowing, reading, buying or talking about a book with a child in your life and spreading the love of reading. We want to make sure the next generation continue to have access to books, wherever they come from.

And if you would like to consider donating to charities that help fund literacy projects, find out more at **www.literacytrust.org.uk** and **www.booktrust.org.uk**.

THANK YOU

*As reported by the National Literacy Trust

INDEX OF FIRST LINES